A STUBBORN FURY

HOW WRITING WORKS IN ELITIST BRITAIN

Gary Hall

The **MEDIA : ART : WRITE : NOW** series mobilises the medium of writing as a mode of critical enquiry and aesthetic expression. Its books capture the most original developments in technology-based arts and other forms of creative media: AI and computational arts, gaming, digital and post-digital productions, soft and wet media, interactive and participative arts, open platforms, photography, photomedia and, last but not least, amateur media practice. They convey the urgency of the project via their style, length and mode of engagement. In both length and tone, they sit somewhere between an extended essay and a monograph.

Series Editor: Joanna Zylinska

A STUBBORN FURY

HOW WRITING WORKS IN ELITIST BRITAIN

Gary Hall

( )

OPEN HUMANITIES PRESS

London 2021

Print ISBN 978-1-78542-092-4
PDF ISBN 978-1-78542-091-7

OPEN HUMANITIES PRESS

Open Humanities Press is an international, scholar-led open access publishing collective whose mission is to make leading works of contemporary critical thought freely available worldwide.

More at http://openhumanitiespress.org

Contents

I have no social class, marginalized as I am. The upper class considers me a weird monster, the middle class worries I might unsettle them, the lower class never comes to me.

Clarice Lispector, Hour of the Star

This is not an autobiography. This genre is forbidden to me.

Pierre Bourdieu, Sketch for a Self-Analysis

I don't want to be included. Instead, I want to question the standard in the first place.

Reni Eddo-Lodge, Why I'm No Longer Talking to White People About Race

Stay Elite

*E*litist Britain, a 2019 report from the Sutton Trust and Social Mobility Commission, found that two fifths (39%) of the country's 'leading people' were educated privately, more than five times as many as in the population as a whole, with almost a quarter (24%) graduating from Oxford or Cambridge (aka Oxbridge). Research by Ofcom (2019), the UK's regulator for communication services, similarly revealed that those working in the television industry were twice as likely to have been educated at a private school than other workers (i.e. 14%, double the national average of 7%), with women, those from minority ethnic groups and disabled people being underrepresented in all roles. Add to this the appearance of books such as Francis Green and David Kynaston's *Engines of Privilege* (2019) and *The Class Ceiling* (2019) by Sam Friedman and Daniel Laurison, and we have a flurry of recent publications showing Britain to be one of the most unequal places in Europe. In *A Stubborn Fury* I examine the effect of such a widespread lack of opportunity on the country's culture, and thus on the way in which the British make sense of themselves. I'm interested in exploring *who* is able to contribute to this culture – and, more importantly, *how* they are able to do so. The latter is an issue that all too often remains unaddressed in studies of privilege and exclusiveness.

Although my subtitle is designed to evoke the Sutton Trust's 2019 report, it is primarily the culture of England I concentrate on, as the relation between class and social mobility is played out differently in the three nations that make up Great Britain: England, Scotland and Wales. We can see this from the data on admissions to the Universities of Oxford and Cambridge that the Labour MP David Lammy accessed through 'Freedom of Information' requests and released in 2017. For Lammy, this 'data clearly shows that a privileged background is still the key to getting through the Oxbridge admissions process … [O]ver 81% of offers were made to the sons and daughters of people in the two top socio-economic classes in 2015, compared to 79% in 2010 and 77% between 2004 and 2009' (Lammy 2017). Further analysis of Lammy's data carried out by the Sutton Trust in 2018 reveals that the South East of England 'had the highest acceptance rate' at Cambridge, 'with 35% of students who applied from the area gaining a place' (Montacute and Cullinane 2018, 12). By contrast, 'in Wales (the area with the lowest acceptance rate) only 26% of students who applied gained a place' at Cambridge, while 'just 19% of students applying to Oxford from Wales were given an offer' (12). Indeed, *Access To Advantage*, the report in which the latter analysis appears, indicates that even within England itself the 'proportion of HE [higher education] applicants from state schools' who are accepted at Oxbridge 'differs substantially by region', the South and East of England diverging markedly from the rest of the country. Approximately '1.5% of HE applicants from the South East, South West, London and East of England went to Oxbridge, but only around 0.8% of those from the North or the Midlands' (3). In his foreword to *Access to Advantage*, Peter Lampl, the founder of the Sutton Trust, acknowledges that geography is a significant barrier faced by people from less advantaged backgrounds who wish to improve their chances of social mobility. 'Depending on where you were born, your access to the best universities can be severely limited' (2). But there is even more to it than that. *Not* attending Oxbridge can also severely restrict one's chances of becoming a published author in the UK. It was found in 2017, for instance, that 44% of the country's poets and novelists were educated at one of those two universities.

In what follows I explore some of the consequences of this inequality – and of the educational uniformity that accompanies it – for English culture. Focusing on the literary novel and memoir, I investigate why so much of the writing produced in England is, to put it bluntly, uncritically liberal, humanist, realist and anti-intellectual. I do so through a playfully performative engagement with two of the most acclaimed contributions to our understanding of these media genres of recent times. One is that of the English novelist and artist Tom McCarthy. I'm especially interested in the importance he attaches to European modernism and antihumanist theory when it comes to appreciating how literature works. The other is that of the French memoirists Didier Eribon and Édouard Louis, and their attempt to reinvent the antihumanist philosophical tradition of Michel Foucault, Hélène Cixous, Bruno Latour *et al.* by producing a theory that speaks about class and intersectionality, yet has the potential to generate the excitement of a Kendrick Lamar concert. The reason I adopt a playfully performative approach, to the point *A Stubborn Fury* is a book not just about Tom McCarthy but also about 'Tom McCarthy', is to push back against the liberal humanist privileging of the unique human author as individual creative genius. I'm thus not positioning *my antihumanist philosophy* in a relation of contrast with that of these competing thinkers, as if we were all involved in a struggle for intellectual dominance over who is right. Instead, I'm endeavouring to enact my theory of how writing works in *A Stubborn Fury* by collaborating critically and creatively *with these authors* in the form of a literary-philosophical repetition, détournment and remix. Experimentally 'pirating' McCarthy, Eribon and Louis in this way, I endeavour to answer that most urgent of questions: what can be done about English literary culture's addiction to the worldview of privileged, middle-class white men, very much to the exclusion of more radically inventive writing, including that of working-class, BAME and LGBTQIAP+ authors?

PART I

Go to Settings (feat. Didier Eribon and Édouard Louis)

CHAPTER I

On Class and Culture in Elitist Britain

During the summer of 2018 I attended an event organised by the London Review Bookshop to mark the publication in English of two celebrated French volumes: *Returning to Reims* by Didier Eribon (2018) and *History of Violence* by Édouard Louis (2018). In Eribon's powerful memoir, the Parisian sociologist travels home for the first time in thirty years following the death of his father, a 'stupid and violent' man he had never loved and had long held in 'contempt' (Eribon 2013, 33).[1] There he tries to account for the shift in politics of his working-class family while he has been away: from supporting the Communist Party to voting for the National Front.

Returning to Reims was a significant influence on Louis, inspiring him to write his bestselling first novel, *The End of Eddy* (2017), which he dedicated to Eribon. Like the latter's memoir, *The End of Eddy* and *History of Violence* both in their different ways tell the story of how the author, having grown up gay and poor in post-industrial northern France, was eventually able to escape his

working-class environment through education. 'I real-
ised that was pretty much the only way I could get away
from my past', Louis writes, 'not just geographically, but
symbolically, socially – that is completely. ... Studying
was the only real escape route I could find' (2018, 74).
(Although they are from different generations, Eribon
and Louis first met at university, the former being a
professor at the time and the latter a student. Together
with Eribon's partner, Geoffroy de Lagasnerie, they are
now close friends.)

As is customary on these occasions, the authors read
from their books and discussed their work and lives,
before participating in a question and answer session
with the audience. In this later part of the evening they
spoke about the transition they had made from the
social realm of the working class to that of the middle
class, with its very different gestures, knowledges and
manners of speech. Recognising that they now had a
foot in both camps, each said the process of reinventing themselves had nonetheless left them feeling they
truly belonged to neither. Arriving in Paris at the age of
twenty, for example, Eribon found it far easier to come
out of the sexual closest and assert his homosexuality
to his new cosmopolitan friends than to come out of the
class closet. It was his working-class origins he found
shameful and embarrassing – and that he lied about.
Yet 'I never came to share the values of the dominant
class', Eribon insists in *Returning to Reims*. 'I always felt
awkward or incensed when hearing people around me
talking scornfully or flippantly about working-class

people and their habits and ways of life. After all, that's where I came from' (29).

Both authors also described how, as a consequence, they were unsure for whom they were actually writing. They may be addressing the question of what it means to grow up in a working-class environment in *Returning to Reims* and *History of Violence*: the profound racism, sexism and homophobia they found there; the violent modes of domination and subjectivation; the social impoverishment; the lack of possibilities that are imaginable, to say nothing of those that are actually realisable. However, they were aware few people from that social class were ever likely to read their books, so could hardly say they were writing *for* them. As Eribon acknowledges in *Returning to Reims*:

> When people write about the working class world, which they rarely do, it is most often because they have left it behind. They thereby contribute to perpetuating the social illegitimacy of the people they are speaking of in the very moment of speaking about them. This happens even if they write with the goal of exposing and critiquing the very status of social illegitimacy to which these people are relegated over and over again, because in writing they take a necessary critical distance, and with it comes the position of a judge or an evaluator. (98)

What really captured my attention during the London Review Bookshop event, though, was the moment Eribon and Louis stressed that what they were trying to achieve with their writing was 'reinvent theory': to produce a theory in which 'something is at stake'. Along with de Lagasnerie, they have described this elsewhere as a theory that engages in order to speak about 'class, exploitation, violence, repression, domination, intersectionality' and yet has the potential to generate the excitement of 'a Kendrick Lamar concert' (de Lagasnerie and Louis 2015; de Lagasnerie in Le Monde in English 2018). Now Eribon is of course the author of a well-known biography of the French philosopher Michel Foucault (1992). Nevertheless their comments on theory struck me: partly because I'm interested in critical theory; but mainly because it's difficult to imagine many English literary writers of a similar stature engaging with the kind of radical thought Foucault and his contemporaries are associated with (Eribon 1994), let alone expressing a desire to reinvent it. Since it draws on concepts such as difference and the unconscious to undermine the idea of the self-identical human subject, that theoretical tradition is often described as antihumanist, or posthumanist, in some of its more recent manifestations.[2] By comparison, English literary culture is predominantly liberal and humanist, seeing education in general, and the reading and writing of literature in particular, as a means of liberating the mind of a rational human individual whose singular identity is more or less unified and consistent with itself. Just listen to the novelist Zadie Smith (Cambridge) articulating what a person is for her. 'When a human being becomes a set of data on a website like Facebook, he or she is reduced,' Smith proclaims:

> Everything shrinks. Individual character. Friendships. Language. Sensibility. In a way it's a transcendent experience: we lose our bodies, our messy feelings, our desires, our fears. It reminds me that those of us who turn in disgust from what we consider an overinflated liberal-bourgeois sense of self should be careful what we wish for: our denuded networked selves don't look more free, they just look more owned. (2010)

Smith is careful to acknowledge that fiction can also reduce humans. Yet there are degrees, as there are with software: 'bad fiction does it more than good fiction', for example, 'and we have the option to read good fiction', she insists (2010).

One explanation given for this difference in philosophical approaches between England and France is that, historically, writers in England have been associated to a large degree with the ruling elite: specifically with public schools, Oxbridge colleges and the tradition of the gentleman as *amateur* scholar. It's a situation that offers a sharp contrast to the cafés, streets and factory gates with which the more overtly political French *intellectual* is associated.[3] Indeed, because English culture tends to be suspicious of radical and abstract ideas (as opposed to the emphasis in France on the universal values of freedom and equality since at least the revolution of 1789), 'the intellectual' is often regarded rather

negatively: as someone who is egotistical and supe-
rior. To be treated positively as an author, scholar, even
an academic in England it's best not to be *too intellectual*. Historians such as Mary Beard (Cambridge) and
Yuval Noah Harari are therefore considered acceptable and taken seriously, as they can write clearly in
'plain English' and communicate with a wider public
– the mythical general reader. Theorists such as Bruno
Latour and Catherine Malabou are not, as England's
elitist culture, ironically enough, regards their philosophy and use of language as too complex for 'real' people
to understand. 'They are all there', runs a recent book
review, 'the first-team of intellectual narcissists and
jargon-mongers: Roland Barthes, Jacques Derrida, Luce
Irigaray, Hélène Cixous et al. … the theoreticians … primarily responsible for turning literary studies into the
heartland of the incomprehensible and irrelevant, and
alienating the ordinary reader' (Bradford 2018). (And
that is in *Times Higher Education*, the UK's weekly magazine for academics.)

This constant policing of the parameters of accept-
ability goes some way toward explaining why the
literary novel in England today is so resolutely humanist. Scottish journalist Stuart Kelly (Oxford) even
takes things so far as to compare it unfavourably to
the 'posthuman novel' that is the TV series *Westworld*.
(I'm drawing on newspaper commentary to show that
mainstream culture in Great Britain is not *entirely* dominated by uncritical liberal humanist thought.) For
Kelly, the modern literary novel and its grasp of life is

'outdated', still constrained as it is by its eighteenth-century origins. Nowhere is this more evident than with its 'unquestioned foundations', based as they are on the idea of the autonomous human subject as protagonist, someone who has an 'intact self', 'cogent agency', 'memories they trust – and can trust – and desires they understand' (Kelly 2016). As Kelly points out:

> Philosophers, psychoanalysts and neuroscientists have all called into question these notions that we cherish – will, self, choice, desire, recollection – but the novel has failed to keep up with these insights. I know myself that I do not know myself, that what I want is not what I choose to want, that the 'me' that was 11 is barely recognisable as the 'me' that is 44.
>
> Some novelists – Will Self [University College School, Hampstead and Oxford] ... Tom McCarthy [Dulwich College and Oxford], Nicola Barker [Cambridge], Lydia Millet, and the much-underrated Nigel Dennis (my copy of *Cards of Identity* is much-thumbed and has a clipping of a review by Hélène Cixous inside it) – have tried, and sometimes succeeded in creating novels where the self is not fixed but fluid, where want is both absence and yearning, where the stories we tell ourselves about ourselves are realised as stories. (16)

It's certainly possible to read the work of Tom McCarthy – to take just one of Kelly's examples – as 'a kind of grand anti-humanist manifesto', as the English novelist himself readily concedes during a conversation with fellow author Lee Rourke. Culture here is not about providing 'a vanity mirror for liberal society to see itself reflected back in the way it wants to see itself' (McCarthy in Rourke and McCarthy 2009). Culture, for McCarthy, should rather 'disrupt' and create trouble. Consequently, 'in order to do what needs to be done you need to reject a certain set of assumptions, certain models of subjectivity', he claims – 'for example, the contemporary cult of the individual, the absolute authentic self who is measured through his or her absolutely authentic feeling' (2009). Yet if McCarthy strives to bring the concept of the discrete, sovereign human subject into question in the content of novels such as *Remainder* and *C*, it's a different matter when it comes to how he himself actually functions as an author. There, for all his interest in antihumanist theory and modernist avant-garde writing, McCarthy serves to sustain, rather than shatter, the liberal humanist model of subjectivity and its preconceptions (McCarthy 2017, 211). This is perhaps most apparent from the manner in which McCarthy, as with his eighteenth-century century predecessors – Richardson, Fielding, Sterne, Smollett (all of them 'affluent, middle class white men', Kelly notes) – continues to act as if his novels are, in the last instance, the original creative expression of his own personality as an absolutely singular and unique individual. At the very least McCarthy considers his subjectivity to be fixed to an extent that allows him to assert the moral right to be identified as the sole *human* author of his written works, and to claim copyright over them on an all-rights-reserved basis as his isolable intellectual property, 'in accordance with the Copyright Design and Patents Act 1988'. (Even the unnumbered pages in a text count, as McCarthy surely knows from his reading of Derrida: *'il n'y a pas de hors-texte'*, and all that.)

In *What Ever Happened To Modernism?*, Gabriel Josipovici (Cheltenham College and Oxford) characterises the pseudo-modernist English novel of the Julian Barnes (City of London School and Oxford) / Martin Amis (Oxford) generation as the product of a literary culture that is determinedly realist, preferring sentimental humanism and readability to the kind of ground-breaking experimentation he associates with European modernism. In their 'petty-bourgeois uptightness', their 'terror of not being in control', their 'desire to boast and to shock', Amis and co. are like 'prep-school boys showing off', he writes (Josipovici 2010).[4] And this may indeed be the case. It may also be the case that to disdain the legacy of modernism – not just 'radical writers' such as Kafka and Beckett, but Bataille and Derrida in philosophy, Freud and Lacan in psychoanalysis, Godard and Lynch in film – 'as if it was just some irritation that got in the way of an ongoing rational enlightenment' is, as McCarthy says, 'ethically wrong and aesthetically rubbish' (McCarthy in Rourke and McCarthy 2009). Still, the cure for English culture's addiction to the worldview of prosperous, middle-class white men – or fear of revolution, the underclass and the other, depending on how you want to look at it – is not as simple as more or better modernism. As Isabel Waidner emphasizes in their anthology *Liberating the Canon*, experimental writing in Britain is predominantly white, bourgeois and patriarchal, with working-class, BAME, LGBTQIAP+ and other 'radically innovative literatures' being marginalised (2018, 7).[5] This is hardly surprising. After all, 7% of the UK population attend private school – that is over 600,000 pupils, double the number of the 1970s – and approximately 1% graduate from Oxford or Cambridge. (To be clear, I'm using the term 'private school' to denote any secondary school that is fee-paying. They are *private* in the sense anyone can open one. This distinguishes them from state schools, which are subject to different rules and regulations. 'Private school' thus encompasses those fee-paying institutions known as 'public schools' – *public* because they were established by statute and acknowledged in law. Strictly speaking, only those 'leading' private secondary schools that are members of the self-selecting Headmasters and Headmistresses Conference are 'public schools'.) Indeed, eight private schools send more pupils to be educated at Oxbridge than the remaining 2894 state schools and colleges combined (see Montacute and Cullinane 2018, 20). Yet in 2017 it was found that 'of the poets and novelists included in *Who's Who* ... half went to private schools; and 44% went to Oxbridge' (Solomon 2018).[6] (The Preface to Josipovici's *What Ever Happened To Modernism?* actually begins: 'The first extra-curricula lecture I attended at Oxford ...') One result of this systematic bias is that British authors of a non-white background published fewer than a hundred titles in 2016 (see Shaffi 2016).

I began this book by referring to social realms that contain a lack of possibilities that are imaginable, let alone achievable. It's worth noting in this context that, of the 11,011 children's books published in the UK in 2018, only 743 had a BAME presence. 7% featured BAME characters and just 4% had a BAME lead character – and that's with BAME pupils making up 33.1% of the school population in England (Centre for Literacy in Primary Education 2019).[7] Nor is it only literary culture that is affected by what Eribon calls the 'terrible injustice' of the 'unequal distribution of prospects and possibilities' (52).[8] Comparable statistics can be provided for the arts, drama, music, business, politics, the law, medicine, the military, the civil service, the media and journalism. 54% of the UK's 'top' news journalists were educated in private schools, for example; while of the 81% who attended university, more than a half were educated at Oxbridge, with a third attending just one institution, Oxford (Sutton Trust 2006).[9] Moreover, 94% of all journalists in the UK are white and as few as 0.2% black (Thurman *et al.* 2016; Thurman 2016). Even when it comes to that most stereotypical of working-class sports, football (which in Louis's first memoir Eddy's father suggests he play to toughen him up), the figures are barely any different. Over half of the England players at the 2018 World Cup in Russia were from BAME backgrounds. Yet there were reportedly only two BAME journalists from English newspapers and press agencies there out of approximately one hundred (Taylor 2018).[10] It's a situation that is only likely to get worse in the coming years, as the economy and society endeavour to recover from the effects of the Sars-CoV-2 outbreak.[11]

In a modest bid to counter the inequality of opportunity in Britain, the Welsh BBC Radio 6 presenter Cerys Matthews has talked about programming less music on her show by artists who have been given a leg up by virtue of attending private school, and more music by people from all walks of life, including women and those with a working-class upbringing (Paine 2018).[12] This makes me wonder: if in the future (to return to Kelly's comments on the posthuman novel) 'we' *do* want to foster a culture in England that is not so liberal and humanist, if, as the climate crisis continues to unfold on the other side of the coronavirus outbreak, we do want to develop an appreciation of life, agency and subjectivity that is more complex and diverse – or at least not quite so outdated and elitist – should we adopt a similar stance? Setting up prizes like the Goldsmiths in order to reward literature that is daring and inventive is all very well. But should we not publish – and perhaps read and cite – fewer texts by people who went to private school or Oxbridge, and more by writers from other, less privileged backgrounds?[13] Should we even have quotas?

CHAPTER 2

Bourgeois Theory

If one consequence of the systematic bias in English culture is an inequality of opportunity, another is its long history of anti-intellectualism. As Alex Renton (Eton) remarks in *Stiff Upper Lip*, by the close of the nineteenth century most public schools were 'determinedly anti-intellectual, for reasons chiefly of snobbery – gentlemen should not be taught the skills of tradesmen' (Renton 2017, 213). Renton goes on to show how these institutions largely taught classics. In 1861 the Clarendon Commission quizzed Oxford undergraduates who had gone to the 'ancient nine' schools (Eton, Charterhouse, Harrow, Rugby, Shrewsbury, Westminster, Winchester, St. Paul's and Merchant Taylors'), and discovered that they 'knew very little of geography, history or science, and had "great deficiencies" even in reading and spelling in English' (132). It's a state of affairs far from confined to the late nineteenth and early twentieth centuries. 'Education at the public schools – and many of the grammar schools that aped them – remained primarily a matter of learning Latin and Greek until the 1950s', Renton observes. 'It was still important in getting scholarships until the 1980s'

(27). (This explains the enthusiasm of Eton College King's Scholar Boris Johnson for quoting Roman and Greek historians – although as a sign he has received the education of the old imperial ruling class doing so also acts as a marker of his membership of the governing elite.) Renton makes a direct connection between the anti-intellectualism of these establishments and that of English public life more generally. So, too, does the author and publisher Leonard Woolf (St Paul's and Cambridge). In his autobiography, published in 1960, Woolf sums up the situation as follows:

> England for considerably more than one hundred years has been the most philistine of all European countries. This, I suspect, is largely due to the public schools, which during the period gradually established a dominating influence on public life and imposed upon the whole nation their prejudices, habits, morals, and standards of value. The public school was the nursery of British philistinism. To work, to use the mind, to be a 'swot', as it was called in my school days, was to become an untouchable (except for the purposes of bullying) in the hierarchy of the public-school caste system. ... Use of the mind, intellectual curiosity, mental originality, interest in 'work', enjoyment of books or anything connected with the arts, all such things, if detected, were violently condemned and persecuted ... [T]his attitude was not confined to the boys; it was shared and encouraged

by nearly all the masters. The intellectual was,
and he [sic] still is today, disliked and despised.
(Woolf 1960, 96-97)

Instead of developing the intellect, the emphasis was
very much on the body and sports. Football, cricket
and rugby were all used 'to define physical and psychological character', as well as to exhaust and otherwise
'distract boys from exploring homosexual relation-
ships', writes Robert Verkaik in *Posh Boys*. The legacy
of this ethos survives to this day. In '2012 and 2016 half
the British Olympic teams came from private schools',
Verkaik notes (2018, 36).[14]

I realise that putting forward such arguments can
come across as blunt, strident, rude even (as perhaps can
comments about antihumanist authors claiming copyright). However, I'm guided here by another aspect of
Eribon and Louis' approach to reinventing theory: their
willingness to be disrespectful. Eribon encapsulates
it best in *Returning to Reims*. Praising the philosopher
Jean-Paul Sartre for having insulted the liberal sociologist Raymond Aron in 1968 for being a 'political and
ideological defender of the bourgeois establishment',
Eribon stresses the importance of 'daring to break with
the conventions of polite academic "discussion" – which
always works in favour of "orthodoxy", and its reliance
on "common sense" and what seems "self-evident" in
its opposition to heterodoxy and to critical thought'
(101). (Think too of how the instruction 'Be kind!' is frequently used today by those in positions of power to
close down criticism.)

In drawing attention to the fact that many writers in England attended private schools and graduated from Oxbridge, I'm not just making a crude and ill-mannered point about class, inequality and exclusiveness, a point that is quite familiar by now in any case.[15] I'm also trying to explain why so much of English culture especially remains doggedly liberal humanist, middle class and anti-intellectual.[16] At the same time I want to suggest that theory can help us to recognise this situation and think it through. Is the idea that we should avoid difficult 'jargon' in order to communicate better with so-called ordinary people *really* so self-evident? Is it not rather an instance of what, echoing Antonio Gramsci, we can call society's manufactured 'common sense', the ideology used to maintain the status quo – and often today to eliminate dissent? Is this one of the reasons we are experiencing an ongoing backlash against theory, not just in journalism and the media but in academia too?[17] (Louis and de Lagasnerie [2015] have written about some of the consequences of the 'defamation campaigns' that have been run in France and elsewhere against figures such as Foucault, campaigns that stretch back to at least the 1980s.)[18]

The reason theory is important and shouldn't be dismissed, no matter how abstract its ideas and how challenging its rhetorical style (and no matter how badly some 'star' theorists have behaved on a personal or professional level), is because of the assistance it offers when it comes to understanding our modes of being and doing in the world, conceiving them differently and changing them. Indeed, for Eribon,

> A theory's power and interest lie precisely in the fact that ... it sets as a goal to allow both individuals and groups to see and to think differently about what they are and what they do, and then, perhaps, to change what they do and what they are. It is a matter of breaking with incorporated categories of perception and established frameworks of meaning, and thereby with the social inertia of which these categories and frameworks are the vectors; after such a break, the goal is to produce a new way of looking at the world and thereby to open up new political perspectives. (53)

That said, it's not my intention to suggest we should all simply read more French theory. I want to join Eribon and Louis in promoting *heterodoxy* and *critical thought*; and I want to do so to the extent of daring to break even with the conventions of theory and what it is currently considered to be. For this tradition of critical thinking (which of course is found in many countries, not just France, and extends from Marxism, feminism and psychoanalysis, through critical analyses of race, gender and sexuality, to science and technology studies, new materialism, accelerationism and beyond), has its own blind spots that lead its proponents to accept certain assumptions as common sense as well.

Many of these blind spots relate to how late-stage capitalism and its technical systems (e.g. social media

such as YouTube, social networks such as Twitter and
Academia.edu, online research portals and discipli-
nary repositories such as Elsevier's PURE and SSRN)
have found ways to incorporate those theorists that
McKenzie Wark (2017) calls 'general intellects', and who
are today typically employed as academics, as opposed
to the public intellectuals of the past like Sartre and
Simone de Beauvoir. (Wark's book *General Intellects*
contains appreciations of twenty-one such schol-
ars, including Wendy Chun, Paul Gilroy [University
College School], and Timothy Morton [St. Paul's and
Oxford].) The point I want to make is not so much that
contemporary intellectual labourers are merely con-
stituent elements of the general intellect or 'social
brain', whose only purpose 'is to keep commodifica-
tion going and profits flowing' (Wark 2017). I don't
deny such *commercially-oriented* theorists are,[19] as Wark
says, also trying to 'find ways to write and think and
even act in and against this very system of commodi-
fication that has now found ways to incorporate even
them' (2017). My argument is that their efforts to do so
contain a number of blind spots – or, perhaps better,
datum points – which limit their 'ability to grasp the
general situation' (Wark 2017).[20] This is especially the
case as far as the bourgeois liberal humanist categories
and frameworks with which they continue to operate
are concerned. For these theorists, too, datum points
such as the unique human author, originality, creativity and copyright are held *in practice* as self-evidently
providing the basis for well-mannered debate. Far from

theory enabling these intellectual labourers to think differently about what they are and what they do, the taking-for-granted of such categories and frameworks leads many of them today to likewise work *in favour of orthodoxy* and the perpetuation of the established order. (I want to stress that in making this argument I am adopting Wark's own methodology here: that of reading such theorists 'against themselves, bringing some of the same critical tactics to bear' on the writings of these general intellects, including Wark herself, in order 'to find their limitations' [2017]. After all, does Wark not acknowledge that the general intellects she focuses on in her book 'remain rather bourgeois thinkers' in some respects [2017]?)

Nor are these 'bourgeois theorists', as we might now call them, the only ones who adhere to the conventions of *polite* critical discussion. When it comes to how they write, think and act, it's a state of affairs that persists even in Eribon and Louis' own bold attempt to reinvent theory.

Chapter 3

Memoirs, Memoirs, Memoirs

The contemporary cult of the authentic self is recognisable in many areas of culture today. It can be detected in the enthusiasm for straight, white, male singer-songwriters such as Lewis Capaldi and Ed Sheeran (Rishworth School), with their ordinary, blokeish, 'I am definitely not a manufactured pop star', images. It's visible in the trend for social media influencers to reveal both their mental health struggles and the 'truth' behind their glamorous selfies (e.g. that to arrive at a single 'spontaneous' Instagram shot requires countless carefully curated attempts). But it's perhaps most apparent in the emphasis on the memoir in both fiction and non-fiction. Here a singular perspective is often used as an entry point to a larger topic. This is because readers are presumed to be able to locate and access a work better if they know something about the author as an individual: their history, biography, personality, feelings and so on.

Just to make it clear I'm not advocating we refuse to read and cite *all* Oxbridge-educated writers (any more than Cerys Matthews is banning *all* music that has been created by artists who've attended private school from her radio programme) – this is not an essentialism for me – I'd like to illustrate the last point with an anecdote from the author and journalist Hadley Freeman (Cambridge Centre for Sixth-Form Studies and Oxford). Discussing ideas for a book with someone in publishing, Freeman found herself being waved away with the recommendation she '"knock out a memoir"' instead. Freeman dutifully 'explained that the idea of sharing my not especially eventful life with a load of strangers made me break out in hives, and suggested instead a non-personal idea.' In response she was told her 'advance would be "five times less than it would for the memoir"' (Freeman 2014). It comes as no surprise to find Freeman *has* now published a memoir (Freeman 2020).

To be fair, memoirs are bucking the trend of the general economic situation for writers, which is that only 5% of them now earn the income Virginia Woolf once argued an author needed to be able to work, 67% of them having earned £10,000 or less in 2018 (Royal Society of Literature 2019). As a result it has long since got to the stage where the world of book publishing has become 'wholly memoir-ified', as Freeman amusingly characterises it. 'Nothing gets a publisher's chequebook out faster than a memoir, to the point that nonfiction books that are ostensibly about a specific subject (butchery, say, or George Eliot) are now styled and sold as memoirs (respectively *Cleaving: A Story of Marriage, Meat, and Obsession* by Julie Powell; and *The Road to Middlemarch*, by Rebecca Mead [Oxford].) ... Make the writer a celebrity and the book will sell itself – ta da!' (Freeman 2014).[21]

It's an aspect of the cult of individual personality that Eribon and Louis appear to have few reservations about as far as its appearance in contemporary literary culture is concerned. Told by Toni Morrison that she can't 'understand this new fashion in literature to write about … one's own life', for instance, Louis replies that he doesn't 'see a problem in writing about oneself and only oneself' (Louis 2019a). His reasoning is that 'no experience is unique, that everything we saw had been lived or would be lived by others'. Louis even goes so far as to say he perceives 'in today's autobiography the possibility of a renewal of literature' (2019a).[22] So the two Frenchmen may have read enough theory to know we can't go outside of language, 'for language has no exterior' (Louis 2018, 110). They are aware that language and culture perform us, in other words: that 'we don't think first and then organise our thoughts into language later on, for language is what allows us to think' (110). They may also be endeavouring to produce a theory that is 'real and exciting' and that, as we saw earlier, speaks about 'class, exploitation, violence, repression, domination, intersectionality' (de Lagasnerie and Louis 2015). (This is part of what makes their attempt to refashion theory so fascinating, as take-up of the latter has also tended to be relatively weak in countries with a strong, pragmatic, leftist tradition that is preoccupied with issues such as poverty and class.)[23] Yet the main way Eribon and Louis are trying to reinvent theory in books such as *Returning to Reims* and *The End of Eddy* (or should that be the main way they are being encouraged, if not indeed *conditioned* and *allowed*, to reinvent theory), is through the creation of a personal journey. It is a personal journey on which, like so many contemporary memoirists, they are prepared to divulge something emotional about themselves, something that is often quite shocking, in order to create a narrative the reader is able to follow, absorb and identify with. (Louis' rape in *History of Violence* is the most obvious and powerful example.) It is as if for them, too, the main thing that is *real* and that can be relied upon in a world of political marketing and spin on the one hand, and distrust of the 'expert' purveyors of objective truth and empirical evidence (journalists, pollsters, government bureaucrats, judges, most academics and politicians) on the other, is the author's own absolutely authentic consciousness and life-experiences.[24] More attention is often paid to who you are and where you come from here than to what you say, with voices on social media constantly being on the lookout for any hint of hypocrisy.

My mention of the expert is a reference to the infamous comment made by Michael Gove (Robert Gordon's College and Oxford) during the 2016 European Union referendum campaign, to the effect that people today have had enough of hearing from them (Mance 2016). (Except, that is, when there's a pandemic to be dealt with. Then it's OK for the government to wheel out a couple of bona fide scientists to stand next to the prime minister.) And, to be sure, an emphasis on the authentic self is often used to explain the attraction for many of the post-truth, post-factual version of politics

associated with Boris Johnson (Eton and Oxford) and
the Brexiteers in the UK and with Donald Trump in
the US. Supposedly anti-establishment figures such as
Johnson, Nigel Farage (Dulwich College) and the forty-
fifth president of the United States are held as offering
something very different to the professional politi-
cal-technocratic class, generally represented in this
narrative by David Cameron (Eton and Oxford), Tony
Blair (Fettes and Oxford), Joe Biden, Barack Obama and
the Clintons. This is despite the fact that both Johnson
and Farage are public-school-educated, while Trump
is the son of a wealthy real-estate developer. The argument is that, because politics is now so marketed and
spun, voters have turned to looking for other clues as to
what politicians *are really like.* Politics has thus become
less about differences of ideology (of which there were
relatively few between David Cameron, Gordon Brown
and Tony Blair, certainly, even if they did represent
opposing political parties), and more about questions
of individual character. Hence the interest shown in
Blair *(not) doing God* and praying with George Bush
prior to the invasion of Iraq; Brown calling Labour-
voting pensioner Gillian Duffy a 'bigoted woman' after
she grumbled to him about immigration; Cameron
revealing his inner Flashman by telling then Shadow
Treasury Chief Secretary Angela Eagle (Oxford) to 'calm
down, dear'; and Theresa May (Oxford) spending nearly
£1,000 on chocolate-coloured leather trousers from
Amanda Wakeley (Cheltenham Ladies' College). The
result is an increasing disenchantment with *politics as*

usual and with the professional politicians of the state, there being little to choose between the different parties in this respect.

Yet one of the reasons Johnson and his ilk have taken liberal commentators by surprise is because character does not appear to matter in their case. Qualities and actions that might once have ended careers – ignorance, arrogance, incompetence, mismanagement, misogyny, bigotry, sexual harassment, extra-marital affairs, the telling of politically incorrect jokes, the incitement of violence against opponents, the showing of a blatant disregard for democracy, the rule of law and the politics of the 'good chap' – only serve to make these political figures *appear* less spun and more authentic, even in their very inauthenticity. The public may well view them as lying, cheating and manipulating their way to power much like any other politician. What sets them apart – in marked contrast to a figure such as Tony Blair, who has still not been forgiven for his duplicitous attitude toward war in Iraq – is that *they are not trying to hide it.* They are just being themselves. (So too was Jeremy Corbyn who – for all his own private education at Castle House Preparatory School – was perceived as being authentic in his own fashion, unlike the professional politician Theresa May. Evidence the nickname she was given: the Maybot.) It's also a tactic that makes Johnson and co. frustratingly difficult for the liberal establishment to engage with on the level of reasoned argument and verified information. After all, they can hardly be shamed as untrustworthy liars if they are quite upfront about being so.

At first glance it might seem that tracing a connection between post-truth politics and the emphasis of Eribon and Louis on the authentic autobiographical self is a bit of a stretch. Yet *The New Yorker* magazine is just one of those cultural institutions to have positioned Louis as an authority on the *gilets jaunes* protesters in France. The magazine did so precisely because the leaderless movement for economic justice is seen as consisting, 'in part, of people like Édouard Louis' family and former neighbors', people who are angry with President Emmanuel Macron and a 'government they feel has both forgotten and exploited them' (Schwartz 2018). They are those who have famously been 'left behind' by globalisation; those people who are still rooted in twentieth-century ideas of nation, place and local identity (as opposed to Theresa May's 'rich citizens of nowhere' who make up the global, metropolitan, liberal elite of the twenty-first century), and who, in the UK and US, are often held as having voted for Brexit, Johnson and Trump against their own class interests. A comment offered in parenthesis by the interviewer from *The New Yorker* is informative in this respect. It reveals just how crucial it is to be able to read Louis' *roman à clef* as a genuine form of personal testimony: 'He has said that everything in the novel [*The End of Eddy*] is true' (Schwartz 2018). It's worth quoting Louis at length from this interview, just to convey the degree of importance that is attached to the authenticity of both *his* feelings and those of the *gilets jaunes*:

> I saw pictures from the movement ... and in those pictures I saw very poor people, people like my mother, people like my father, exhausted people, extremely poor people. I was able to read it on their faces, because I know those people. I recognized, suddenly, a *body,* in the noblest sense of the term. A body that I'm not used to seeing in the media. And I felt that these images were crying out to me. ...
>
> It's the body of social exclusion. It's the body of poverty. It's the body of people who are living in precarity ... Maybe you have to really come from that world to immediately identify it.
>
> Actually, when I started to write books, it was because I had the impression that these kinds of bodies were never depicted. And, when I was a kid, my parents, and especially my mother, always said, 'No one is talking about us. No one cares about us'. One of the most violent feelings we had was this feeling of not existing in the public discourse, in the eyes and voices of others. It was like an obsession. There was not *one* day where my mother didn't say, 'No one is talking about us. The whole world could care less'. And so, for example, elections were the moment when she tried to fight against that kind of invisibility. Voilà. (Louis in Schwartz 2018)

In fact both Louis and Eribon are celebrated for an ability that has been bestowed on them precisely by their autobiographical backstories (an ability most other writers on this account lack, since, as we know, writers from lower socio-economic and working-class backgrounds are very much the exception). I'm referring to their capacity to understand the feelings of the *left behind* on a personal, even bodily level. They then use this understanding to explain why, across Europe and beyond, the politics of this section of society have swung so violently from supporting parties of the left to supporting the populism and nationalism of the far right. Eribon in particular portions a 'heavy measure of responsibility' for the latter process to the official left wing and its own shift rightwards over the course of the eighties, nineties and two thousands. It's a shift that is apparent in the preoccupation of party leaders – many of whom were not working class themselves – with achieving a neoliberal revolution (2013, 126). In the UK this change was initially to be brought about for Blair through the adoption of a third way between left and right in order to champion the (neoliberal) modernisers over the traditionalists. In France it's a transition that has led to the 'neither left nor right' centrism of Macron and his privileging of so-called progressives against conservatives. Granted, this move rightwards brought with it electoral success for the left. The problem, according to Eribon, is that

> The parties of the left, along with party intellectuals and state intellectuals, began from

this moment forward to think and speak the language of those who govern, no longer the language of those who are governed. They spoke in the name of the government (and as part of it), no longer in the name of the governed (and as part of them). And so of course they adopted a governing point of view on the world, disdainfully dismissing (and doing so with great discursive violence, a violence that was experienced as such by those at whom it was directed) the point of view of those being governed. (2013, 129-130)

The result is the electoral fight against this dismissal and the associated sense of invisibility that Louis describes both his mother and the *gilets jaunes* protesters as engaging in. (It is surely no coincidence that the yellow vests that serve as a symbol of this movement and provide it with its name function to make these people extremely visible.)

As far as Eribon and Louis are concerned, the personal lens through which they describe what it feels like to be them and regale their readers with real-life stories of the struggles they have overcome to get where they are and of how that process, that journey, has *changed* them (which is such a characteristic feature of today's memoirified culture), provides a means of engaging critically with the professional neoliberal politicians of both the left and the right. It enables the two memoirists to recount their intimate experience of those 'people who have been socially dispossessed and geographically excluded'; and to do so as authentic ex-members of this social group – ex-members who nonetheless continue to have one foot in this world (Louis in Schwartz 2018). For Tom McCarthy, by contrast, the kind of emphasis Eribon and Louis place in their writings on realism, on readability, and especially on the absolutely genuine expressive self, is 'not just a bad aesthetic model', it is also the 'cultural wing of the whole neo-liberal project'. As he provocatively counters:

> Blair can turn up in front of a committee after having overseen blatant contraventions of every which law imaginable, and get off scot-free by saying he authentically, genuinely felt that invading Iraq was the right thing to do. Like, who gives a shit what he felt? He did X, Y and Z: off to prison! ...
>
> It's not some coincidence that the frameworks of consumer society are absolutely attuned to this type of aesthetic. Express yourself by purchasing our products. (McCarthy in Rourke and McCarthy 2009)

Yet, as we shall see, for all his professed antihumanism and critique of consumerism, McCarthy is far from being able to elude such frameworks himself.

PART II

HOW LITERATURE
WORKS © Tom McCarthy

CHAPTER 4

This is *All* Pirated

McCarthy is especially interesting in this context, as he is often held up as England's leading avant-garde novelist. Like the authors of *Returning to Reims* and *History of Violence*, McCarthy has read enough theory to know it is language and writing that perform us more than it is us who perform language and writing. In *Transmission and the Individual Remix*, his short non-fiction ebook on how literature works, McCarthy draws on Aeschylus' *Oresteia* trilogy (oh, those public school boys and their classics!) to make the point that 'information – and, by extension perhaps, language itself – is no abstract, natural phenomena: it's a manufactured, mediated, and material *regime* in which we find ourselves, the precursor and precondition to our agency and actions ... we are always not just ... *in medias res*, i.e., in the middle of events, but also simply in media. In the beginning is the signal' (McCarthy 2012).

Initially at least, McCarthy appears open to taking on board the implications of this philosophy of media for how he composes his literary fiction and non-fiction. Whereas Eribon and Louis are very much concerned to relate their own, authentic, human consciousness and experience in their books, writing for McCarthy is far from being the original creative expression of a unique authorial subject. Writing is about transmission; it's about broadcasting signals that have no origin. McCarthy does not consider himself to be the originator of 'his' texts, in other words: he is 'their repeater whose composing consists first and foremost of listening' (2012). The result is an 'endless feedback' loop in which 'speaking is listening to speaking', which is in turn 'listening – round and round … For Cocteau, as for Heidegger', and now for McCarthy, 'speaking, real speech, the speech of poets and philosophers, is listening – and speaking-as-listening is repetition.' The only option for the writer in this situation is to be a 'receiver, modulator, transmitter: a remixer' (2012).

In another book of literary criticism, *Tintin and The Secret of Literature*, McCarthy thus rewrites Nicolas Abraham and Maria Torok's own rewriting of Freud's 'The Wolf Man' in their *The Wolf Man's Magic Word* (2006). McCarthy then rewrites the story of Sergei Pankajev (i.e. the Wolf Man) a further time with the character of Serge Carrefax in his novel *C*. This scattering of signals and identities over time and space, and the gathering-together of them again to create something new – something that is in fact 'radically old' – is just how literature works (McCarthy 2012).[25] As he explains in his book on Tintin: 'All literature is pirated. Good literature is constantly expropriated, reappropriated and remade – both by other writers *and* by readers.' (I'll come back to this idea of *good literature*, which we also saw in Smith.) 'Every act of reading is its own kind of remaking of a work' (2006). (And in case you hadn't noticed already, this is exactly what I'm doing here: I'm *pirating* McCarthy's words in order to perform a repetition, a modulation, a 'détournement'. The latter, he tells us, 'involves the taking over of a sign, image, text or body of work and the redirecting of it to one's own ends' [2006].)

McCarthy has acquired this rejection of liberal society's dominant humanist explanation of what it is to write and read literature from the legacy of the twentieth-century avant-garde and high-modernist experimentation. And he considers theory to be an integral part of this legacy. So much so that, as far as he is concerned:

> When an author tells you that they're not beholden to any theory, what they usually mean is that their thinking and their work defaults, without even realizing it, to a narrow liberal humanism and its underlying – and reactionary – notions of the (always 'natural' and preexisting, rather than constructed) self, that self's command of language, language as a vehicle for 'expression' ... When [Alain Robbe-Grillet] decries, in *Towards a New Novel*, the tendency of cultural journalists to use the term 'avant-garde' to sideline books that don't conform to a system – and it *is* a system, with its histories and its contingencies, its ideological buttressing and so on – of sentimental naturalism,

> Robbe-Grillet could be speaking for myself or
> any other contemporary writer who refuses to
> reassert this clapped-out system's values. These
> values, and this system, can lead nowhere else
> but to the middle-brow commercial novel –
> which, in turn, does nothing else than reassert
> them. (2012)

It therefore comes as no surprise to find McCarthy's work described as 'one of contemporary prose fiction's most urgent and innovative pleas for the continued relevance' of theory (Nieland 2012, 578). Alongside his willingness to critique liberal humanism and his own association with the avant-grade, this commitment to theory is another of the reasons I've chosen to concentrate on his writing here (as opposed to that of Nicola Barker, say, or Will Self). For McCarthy, it's important we persist in listening to theory and repeating its lessons.

Pursued without reserve, McCarthy's antihumanism would certainly be capable of creating trouble: for the expressive self of the fiction and non-fiction memoir, but also for many of the categories and frameworks that are associated with consumer society. Interestingly, the latter include those relating to copyright and the question of rightful ownership that, as we have seen, ultimately lead McCarthy to function as a reactionary liberal humanist himself. The whole of the last chapter of *Tintin and The Secret of Literature*, for example, is given over to the topic of pirates and piracy. Here, in what is the book's final section, McCarthy demonstrates that he is well aware of contradictions such as the fact the 'estate of James Joyce, who saw "literature" itself as rich trash to be recycled and adapted … is positively draconian when it comes to authorising adaptations or allowing access to material' (2006). The estate of T.S. Eliot, 'who made a career out of reusing other people's lines', likewise 'stamps down on any citation of his work that exceeds the amount the letter of the law allows' (2006). Yet it's notable that McCarthy neglects to build on this awareness to consider the implications of the potential challenge that antihumanist theory and the notion that we are always *in* language and *in* media offer to late stage capitalism and its ideas of copyright and piracy. The most we get in this respect are those comments that come immediately after what he says about Joyce and Eliot. Academics rail at this contradictory situation and 'cry for changes in the copyright laws', McCarthy writes. 'Artists, meanwhile, do what artists always did: steal. Perhaps when the end of *Tintin's* protection era comes the period will be viewed nostalgically by creative people who want to base their work on Hergé's as a golden age, a time when it still had the *frisson* of illegality. The really savvy ones are not bothering themselves about that now, though: if they have any sense they are involving themselves in the planning of an opera set to open on 3 March 2053. Its title? *The Castafiore Emerald*' (2006). McCarthy doesn't therefore reject or disrupt the distinction between exclusive ownership and illegal theft as it relates to copyright law. Instead he sidelines the issue – in part, by projecting it into a fictional future where it will no longer be against the law to copy, modify, reuse, translate, distribute and make derivative versions of Hergé's work without permission. (The remaining paragraphs of *Tintin and The Secret of Literature* are devoted to a scene-by-scene description of the 2053 opera of his imagination.)

While he may be mindful of the contingency of 'natural' processes of moral right, McCarthy's approach to piracy is a moralistic one nonetheless. He clearly knows what piracy is *in advance* of any theoretically-informed intellectual questioning: piracy for him is associated with lifting and stealing the work of others. By contrast, I would maintain that a responsible ethical (as opposed to moralistic) approach to piracy – of a kind that would be in keeping with McCarthy's insistence on the continued relevance of radical thought – would *not* presume to know what it is in advance. Rather, the question of piracy would remain far less clear-cut and much more open and undecided. Elsewhere I have explained what I mean by this by showing how the issue of piracy can be understood in relation to the concept of the legislator in Jean-Jacques Rousseau's *The Social Contract*. Is the legislator, the founder of a new law or institution, legitimate or a charlatan? We can never know. And the reason we can never know is because of 'the aporia that lies at the heart of authority, whereby the legislator already has to possess the authority the founding of the new institution is supposed to provide him or her with in order to be able to found it' (Hall 2016, 141). My argument, developed with reference to a range of examples, from

Napster and The Pirate Bay, through Google Books to
Aaron Swartz and the Aaaaarg shadow library, is that:

> Certain so-called Internet pirates are in a sim-
> ilar situation to Rousseau's legislator. They
> too may be involved in performatively invent-
> ing, trialing, and testing the very new laws and
> institutions by which their activities may then
> be judged and justified. As such, they can claim
> legitimacy only from themselves. This is a state
> of affairs that as well as marking their impos-
> sibility also constitutes their founding power,
> their instituting force. It is here, between the
> possible and the impossible, legality and ille-
> gality, that we must begin any assessment or
> judgment of them. And it should be noted that
> it is not just the potential pirates who may
> be legislators or charlatans. The current laws
> and institutions by which we might condemn
> Internet piracy as illegal are based on the same
> aporetic structure of authority. Such lawmak-
> ers are always also undecidably charlatans or
> pirates too. (141)[26]

McCarthy's moralistic attitude, however, means that –
almost in spite of himself and his own self-conscious
intellectualism – he is unable to keep the question of
piracy open to an extent that would enable him to think
further about its many contradictions and ambiguities
in terms other than legal vs. illegal. Instead of drawing
on his reading of continental philosophy to interrogate society's normative assumptions about rightful

ownership and authorship critically, McCarthy defaults to them 'without even realizing it' (2012). Academics adhere to the law at the same time as demanding it be changed, while artists such as 'Bosch, Michelangelo, Renoir, Monet, Picasso – steal anything in sight' (2006). It's a set of taken-for-granted conventions that, as well as *naturally* providing the basis for polite critical discussion, clearly support capitalism's consumer culture. As McCarthy intimates with regard to the estates of James Joyce, T.S. Eliot and Hergé himself, deeming certain forms of 'pirate' activity as stealing and hence punishable as a criminal act is obviously hugely beneficial for the producers and owners of intellectual property rights (who are *undecidably charlatans and pirates* themselves, I would insist). It also brings with it the additional benefit of simultaneously undermining those *artists-cum-pirates* that, although unacknowledged by McCarthy, *are* taking the risk of trying to develop alternatives to capitalism's predatory systems of property. These pirates are doing so by operating in a manner that is neither simply legitimate nor illegitimate, legal nor illegal, in order to rethink ideas of copyright, possession, reproduction and controlled distribution: say, in terms of a common stock of shared resources that everyone is free to access and use, in the case of shadow libraries such as Aaaaarg, UbuWeb and Memory of the World.[27]

The impression McCarthy gives of being rather conservative in this respect is compounded by the fact he does little to disturb or otherwise cause trouble for copyright law when it comes to his own activities as an author. His ideas of transmission and remix may lead him to associate the composition of literature with piracy and theft. (Along with his references to the likes of Heidegger and Robbe-Grillet, this is one of the things that makes his work so stimulating intellectually, certainly when compared to the majority of English novelists writing today.) Yet it's noticeable that McCarthy is loath to go so far as to 'steal' anything himself, in the sense of actually risking the infringement of copyright as it currently stands by trialling or testing the law in order to bring its notions of what is legal and illegal radically into question. (In his novel *Men In Space* he is careful to acknowledge where the extracts from 'Papa Won't Leave You Henry' by Nick Cave and the Bad Seeds, 'Stephanie Says' by The Velvet Underground, and 'Back in the USSR' by The Beatles are taken from, and who the all rights reserved copyright holders are of the lyrics he quotes by Nick Cave, Lou Reed, and John Lennon and Paul McCartney.) The kind of piracy McCarthy is referring to a lot of the time is just what every *great* writer does. 'There is nothing "new" about this', he emphasises. Remix is thus *not* a quintessentially digital phenomenon for him as it is for a lot of others who associate it with using new technology to copy, edit and recombine pre-existing images, music and text. 'Shakespeare was remixing Ovid, Plutarch, Holinshed, not to mention the authors of the *King Leirs* and *Hamlets* already in circulation when he penned his versions' (2012). It is far from obvious that such remixing *should* even be considered stealing – although the estates of Joyce and Hergé might argue otherwise.

Nor is copyright the only conceptual datum point that ultimately leads McCarthy to work in support of a continuation of the accepted order, even though his writing definitely has the potential to push us toward reconceiving those norms with which the novelist conventionally operates. (It is this potential that makes his work so exciting and suggestive for me.) There are numerous others. They include the individual human author, the named proprietorial subject, the proper signature, writing, the book, the novel published with a brand-name press, the finished artefact, immutability, linear thought, the long-form argument and the single-voiced narrative. Yet McCarthy is far from alone in functioning like this. In other writings I have discussed some of these datum points as they apply to the creation, publication and dissemination of theory more generally (Hall 2016; 2017). For even today it's difficult to think of a well-known French philosopher or theorist who has not made their name by publishing *serious* codex print monographs that are made available for sale on a copyrighted basis.

Here, though, I want to draw attention to the fact that McCarthy is unwilling to follow the logic of the antihumanist theory with which he is associated – and with which he regularly associates himself – so far as to actually discard, dislodge or even interrogate rigorously those datum points his work habitually relies upon. ('What do I do?', asks the narrator of his 2015 novel *Satin Island*: 'I am an anthropologist ... symbolic operations lying on the flipside of the habitual and the banal: identifying these, prising them out and holding then up, kicking and wriggling to the light – that's my racket' [2015b, 15-16].) Admittedly, following such logic might eventually lead McCarthy to undermine the privilege afforded to the autonomous author, to writing as the definitive information behaviour, and to the book as fixed and finished material object, in favour of systems of signals that do indeed repeat, pulse and mutate. It's quite possible, then, that it would see him approach the place 'at which the writing's entire project crumples and implodes' – to borrow the words of his *Typewriters, Bombs, Jellyfish* essay collection – and he has to begin to invent (and perhaps even be performatively part of) very different means of creating, publishing and disseminating art and culture (2017, 70). Yet as Eribon and Louis invite us to reflect, isn't this why theory is so important: because it helps us to acknowledge the consequences of our thinking and to take the risk inherent in doing so, namely, that it might change us and our own ways of being and doing in the world quite radically?

That McCarthy is one of the few English writers to point us in this direction is without doubt a large part of what makes his work so valuable in the contemporary context. Nevertheless, instead of following this path himself (and I'm again recycling his words from *Typewriters, Bombs, Jellyfish*), McCarthy continues to reassert the moral and legal right to be recognised as the original author of his novels, and thus as an 'autonomous, autarchic self … in the form of the artist who masters his craft, works its machinery with delicacy and precision so as to both express himself and turn the world into a set of works' (211). It is a set of works that, in his desire for authority and prestige, McCarthy signs 'triumphantly with his own proper name' on the basis that they are indeed *all his*.[28] He then proceeds to give them over to professional for-profit publishers in what he insists is their fixed and final integral form, so that they can be made available for sale on the market under an all rights reserved license as clearly distinguishable consumer products. His debut novel *Remainder*, for instance, written in 2001, was originally published in November 2005 by the Paris-based art publisher Metronome Press, McCarthy having taken some time to find a home for it. *Remainder* was subsequently republished: first in 2006 by the independent UK press Alma Books and then again in 2007 by Vintage Books in the US. The latter is an imprint of Knopf, which is owned by Penguin Random House, the largest publisher of general interest paperbacks in the world. Penguin Random House is in turn jointly owned by the British global publishing company Pearson PLC and the German media conglomerate Bertelsmann. McCarthy's novels *C* and *Satin Island* were both published by Vintage too, in 2010 and 2015 respectively, as in 2012 were *Transmission and the Individual Remix* and an updated edition of McCarthy's second novel, *Men in Space*. Clearly, then, McCarthy's performance of his own authorial identity cannot be positioned in a relation simple of contrast and opposition to that of the rational, opportunity-maximising, self-interested subject of late stage capitalism.

The assertion of copyright on McCarthy's part means that it is not just the scaffolding of consumer society he has problems disrupting to any significant degree. As I showed earlier, he is unable to cause much trouble for liberal humanism's worn-out model of subjectivity as well. (Remember, this is the very reactionary conception of the self McCarthy portrays his antihumanism as challenging.) Indeed, the reason I keep coming back to copyright is because of its close connection with the production of liberal humanist agency and subjectivity. Copyright, as Mark Rose emphasises, 'is not a transcendent moral idea, but a specifically modern formation [of property rights] produced by printing technology, marketplace economics *and the classical liberal culture of possessive individualism*' (Rose 1993, 142; my emphasis). In this respect our current copyright laws have at least a dual function. They protect the author's economic and moral rights, as is generally understood. But – and this is something that is less frequently appreciated – they also participate in creating and shaping the author as a *sovereign, liberal, human subject*.

As a consequence, it is extremely difficult to avoid defaulting to the clapped-out system of liberal humanism – and, with it, the morals and prejudices of the bourgeois, patriarchal establishment. This is the case even for those who, operating under the influence of antihumanist theory, *are* explicitly interested in doing

so. Certainly McCarthy's denunciation of the traditional liberal humanist conception of what it is to be an
author in favour of a modulation of writing as an imper-
sonal process of remixing is insufficient to ensure he
escapes this fate. In fact, McCarthy continues to reaffirm this system and its underlying hierarchical values
with his version of the remix; for it turns out that not
'any old remix will do'. Instead, there are 'good ones and
bad ones' (2012).

CHAPTER 5

Good and Bad Remixes, or The Importance of Having the Right Software

To be fair, the idea that there are good and bad remixes is fairly common within remix culture. In *This Is Not a Remix*, Margie Borschke shows how 'a judgment about what constitutes a "good" remix' is a prominent feature of legal scholar Lawrence Lessig's well-known book from 2008, *Remix* (Borschke 2017, 59). Borschke makes her point by quoting Lessig's insistence that: '"Remixed media succeed when they show others something new; they fail when they are trite or derivative"' (Lessig 2008, 82). For Lessig, '"good" remixes build new meaning by playing with the meaning of old' (Borschke 2017, 59). By referring to the example of dance music, however, Borschke is able to demonstrate that remixes are by definition derivative. 'They are a new version' (59). This means they can't be divided into good and bad on the basis of whether they are new, original and transformative – or not.

In *Transmission and the Individual Remix* McCarthy brings a similarly judgemental approach to bear on the issue of what constitutes a good remix. He offers William Burroughs as an example of a good remixer, comparing his remixes favourably to those of Brion Gysin and Tristan Tzara:

> Why does Burroughs conjure so much more richness from the same source material? Because ... he has uploaded the right verbal remix software. He has read and memorized his Dante, his Shakespeare, his Eliot – to such an extent that his activity as a composer consists of giving himself over to their cadences and echoes, their pulses, codas, loops, the better that these may work their way, through him, *The New York Times* and any other body thrown into the mix, into an audibility that ... transforms all of the mix's elements ... (2012)

Only those remixers who have the right software, the right *craft*, the right *techné*, to use the term favoured by Heidegger, can produce good writing, it seems. And, for McCarthy, the right remix software consists largely of those pulses and cadences that are to be found in the classics of Western literature: the works of Dante, Shakespeare, T.S. Eliot *et al.* Yet as Borschke insists (again quoting Lessig), 'the idea that it takes "extraordinary knowledge of a culture" to remix (or to listen) well' (Borschke 2017, 60) doesn't necessarily apply. Drawing again on her knowledge of music culture, popular dance music in particular, she argues that while those remixers

who have a highly trained ear and are experienced at playing records to a dance floor are no
doubt going to be better equipped to make good
decisions about what aspects of song to alter or
rearrange in order to find a new groove in the
mix, there is nothing about the technique per se
that requires knowledge about anything other
than the song being remixed and the technology
used to do that. ... Complexity does not make a
cultural phenomenon better or more valuable; it
only makes it more complex. (60-61)[29]

Famously, for Foucault, one of the risks of announc-
ing the death of the author, as Barthes does, is that the
privilege afforded to this figure is sustained in a different fashion: by means of the *idea* of *the work*. 'The word
work and the unity that it designates are probably as
problematic as the status of the author's individual-
ity', Foucault writes (1984, 104). We have already seen
how the concept of the work continues to be extremely
relevant to the manner in which McCarthy functions
as an author. Does his version of writing as remixing constitute yet another means of imposing liberal
society's standards and values onto literature? Rather
than rejecting or contesting the distinction between
good and bad literature (let alone that between literature, with its special status, and other, more 'ordinary'
forms of writing and communication), is McCarthy not
merely transferring the notion of 'good' away from its
association with the virtuoso author as creative genius,
and onto the remix and remixer? This would certainly

explain why, although remix culture is generally associated with democratising cultural expression and
undermining the idea of the canonical masterpiece –
Matthew Arnold's 'best which has been thought and
said' (Arnold 1869, 5) – very little changes in this respect
as a result of McCarthy's emphasis on the writer as
receiver, modulator, transmitter. After all, reappropriating
the work of others is for him just what every *great* author
does. So it should come as no surprise that, even though
he is endeavouring to provide something of an antihumanist analysis of how literature works, it's almost
invariably those writers who are already accepted as
part of the established canon who are perceived as being
good by McCarthy and located at the top of the cultural
hierarchy. The difference is that now they are privileged
because they are good transmitters of the right signals
and texts, rather than good creators of original authorial expressions. Remixing is not being understood here
as challenging conventional hierarchies of authority to
produce a new, more horizontal and democratic model
of creativity and communication. Indeed, McCarthy
insists that, although the activity of these exceptional
writers is a 'secondary one', in that it is repeating what
they have already been provided with, it is secondary
for him 'in a universe that, truly speaking, has no origin
... Which means, paradoxically, that in being *absolutely*
secondary – that is, in carrying the logic of secondariness to its most extreme configuration – they achieve a
kind of primacy within this universe' (2012).

To be clear, I'm not suggesting that judgements *cannot* be made about authors and works, if these are the contingent categories with which we decide to operate.[30] None of this is a matter of simple relativism for me. I'm just trying to show how it is that, for all his interest in radical theory and in critiquing liberal society and its preconceptions, the conclusions McCarthy reaches as to which remixers and remixes are *good* are much the same as those of the literary status quo. I'm trying to elucidate why, despite his awareness that such systems of judgement are manufactured and contingent rather than natural, McCarthy still arrives at a situation where he can assert Joyce is unconditionally the 'twentieth century's best novelist', and *Krapp's Last Tape* 'the best play written, or rewritten, since *King Lear*' (2012). And where, by the same token, Hergé *cannot* be considered to be a writer of great literature, even though the *Tintin* comics are full of 'significance, intensely associative, overwhelmingly suggestive', because the medium of comics 'still occupies a space below the radar of literature proper' (2006).[31] For we can now see that giving oneself over to the loops and codas of the *great books* of the Western tradition does not necessarily a good remix make. It only *appears* to do so if you adhere to those systems of value that consider this to be the right remix software to begin with.

Ultimately, then, McCarthy's antihumanist account of how writing and literature work is far from radical or transgressive. He actually has a quite conservative and, indeed, humanist appreciation of what a good piece of writing (i.e. remixing) is. Exactly how humanist is apparent from the way in which literary discourses continue to be recognised as such only when they are 'endowed with the author function' (Foucault 1984, 109). McCarthy still treats good writing as being the creation of named, biographical human subjects, in the sense that the person with the proper name Joyce is more or less the same self-identical person to whom *Ulysses* and *Finnegan's Wake* can both be attributed.[32] Tellingly, he fails to treat good writing as the product of anonymous *flows* of signs and signals; or, indeed, as emerging from different (including spatially and temporally different) 'posthuman' assemblages of human and nonhuman intra-actors, where the latter include information media technologies such as language, writing, the school, the university and the codex print book. (It is toward a *posthuman* reading of this kind that I am edging here, very much with the help of those texts signed 'Tom McCarthy'). McCarthy may be critical of the cult of the individual – a cult that lies behind both liberalism and capitalism. Nevertheless, he frequently turns to the biography of the individual person named Hergé for his interpretation of the *Tintin* books. What is more, he does so despite knowing full well that Hergé produced two of his volumes, *The Seven Crystal Balls* and *Prisoners of the Sun*, in close collaboration with another cartoonist, Edgar Jacobs – to the extent the latter requested the books be co-signed. It was a request Hergé refused in order to keep the myth of his single authorship intact. Even before his collaboration with

Jacobs, Hergé employed a sizable number of assistants who 'became so good at drawing his characters that the difference between his own rendition and theirs grew indiscernible', McCarthy notes. 'Right to the end', however, 'he signed the books "Hergé" rather than "Studios Hergé" – and let it be widely understood that, whereas "Disney" denoted a huge corporate operation, "Hergé" meant him and only him'" (McCarthy 2006).

McCarthy's cultural conservativism is apparent in other ways, too. They include, perhaps most obviously, the fact that by far the vast majority of those (re)writers McCarthy considers *good* are male. The list of thirty-five suggestions for further reading he provides at the end of *Tintin and The Secret of Literature* contains only texts written by men (with the partial exception of *The Wolf Man's Magic Word*, which Nicolas Abraham co-authored with Maria Torok). Likewise McCarthy's top ten European modernists: all men (2007).[33] Even Kraftwerk, with whose song 'Antenna' McCarthy opens *Transmission and the Individual Remix*, is an all male band.

CHAPTER 6

Who Speaks, Who Gets to Experiment and What Remains

At this point a question arises that has a number of implications for those interested in the future of the avant-garde novel. Given that McCarthy defaults to a narrow liberal humanism with regard to how he himself operates as an author, and given that liberalism is for him a system and set of values that *can lead nowhere else but to the middle-brow commercial novel*, does that mean the latter judgement can be applied to his own literary fiction?

After all, the writer for McCarthy, as for Roland Barthes in 'The Death of the Author', is a node in a communication network: '*Who speaks?* For Barthes, the answer is always: language – language speaks me, you, everyone, to such an extent that I and you and we and they are merely shifting and amorphous points, floating islands being continuously made and unmade by language's flows and counterflows' (McCarthy 2012). It's a reading of art as the product of a network of transmissions, rather than the original creation of a unique human self, that McCarthy also explores in his activities with the International Necronautical Society (INS), the semi-fictitious avant-garde organization he co-founded with philosopher Simon Critchley. (McCarthy's title is General Secretary, Critchley's that of Chief Philosopher.) In 2004, for instance, the INS set up a functioning radio station in the gallery of London's Institute of Contemporary Art. Over forty assistants proceeded to generate 'poem codes' that were broadcast over FM radio. This was followed in 2008 and 2009 by exhibitions in Germany and Sweden in which black box recorders of fallen aircraft were replicated and used to send out a stream of similar messages. As McCarthy writes of the 2009 installation at the Hartware MedienKunstVerein art institute in Dortmund, this was an INS 'transmission made by doing no more than recombining sequences of words picked up from other radio stations with phrases from local newspapers, medical texts about auditory hallucination, and the odd line of Hölderlin and Shakespeare – and, of course, Ovid. Like Orpheus, or Cégeste, we listened and repeated, while world did its thing' (2012).

Yet it's interesting that McCarthy is unwilling to let the idea we are spoken by language impact on his own (some might say rather clichéd) manner of functioning as a literary novelist to any great extent.[34] He refuses to put his money where his mouth is – quite literally when it comes to his complicity with the corporate publishing world and proprietorial claims to copyright – and question the traditions of his medium by enacting the *death* of the humanist author. '[I]t's not like I set out to write an anti-humanist manifesto', he says to Lee Rourke. 'All I set out to do is make good art. It's really simple' (2009). In fact, far from radically reconceiving the prevailing liberal humanist conception of authorial agency and subjectivity, McCarthy seems more concerned to substitute the realist novelist with a modulated reenactment of the modernist writer (even if 'the modern' for him extends as far back as Aeschylus' *The Oresteia* and Ovid's *Orpheus*).

I stipulate *modulated reenactment* of the modernist writer because it's more than just the logic of antihumanist theory that McCarthy is averse to pursuing with any real degree of conviction. A similar reluctance to confront the implications of his ideas is detectable with regard to his relation to the multiple legacies of the historical avant-garde. It's noticeable that McCarthy does not allow this legacy to impact on his writing to the extent of actually producing a distinctly experimental novel. He may be positioned as the English-language's foremost avant-gardist, his fiction associated with the posthuman (and admired by star theorists in the field such as N. Katherine Hayles), and his non-fiction filled with references to Kathy Acker, Georges Bataille and Stéphane Mallarmé. Nevertheless, neither *Remainder*, nor *C*, nor *Satin Island* are especially avant-garde. In fact it might be said they only appear so when set in the context of the realism that has long dominated the Anglophone literary world. That his work *is* frequently described as avant-garde serves to show just how tame a lot of literature has become.[35] Even McCarthy thinks the contrast between 'lyrical realism' and the avant-garde of his own writing 'doesn't hold' (McCarthy in Kachka 2015). Truth be told, he continues to adhere to many of the conventions of realism that are such a dominant feature of England's resolutely non-modernist, intellectually conservative and highly commercialised literary culture. McCarthy has a fairly formulaic style, using shortish, structurally simple sentences of the kind that are generally aligned with 'good' writing these days. And while some of the ideas contained in his novels are very different from those ordinarily associated with a humanist appreciation of life and subjectivity – I'm thinking of his replaying of mid-century cybernetics in *C*, and of how the discontinuous 'hero' of *Remainder* has 'lost the functionalities that nonconscious cognition performs' (Hayles 2017, 87) – the manner in which he dramatises them is not. As fellow novelist Garth Risk Hallberg observes, all too often McCarthy does so in much the same fashion as Cervantes in *Don Quixote*: 'embody them in a character' and 'launch him' into a continuous linear plot that builds '(albeit one that ends in a Borgesian loop)'. Some 'artful stammerings, elisions, and self-corrections' aside, the first-person narrator of McCarthy's novels is likewise (contra Kelly) still very much a 'consistent, confessional, Cartesian (if unusually estranged) "I"' (Hallberg 2011).[36]

Regardless of his references to the archive of modernist experimentation, McCarthy's is actually quite a traditional version of the novel, then, one that would be reasonably familiar to George Eliot and even

Jane Austen. Similarly, when it comes to the material practicalities of publishing, he is far from being the 'theoretical fundamentalist' Zadie Smith (2009) presents him as. In his questioning of 'the status of literature within culture', he declines to contest the established form and protocols of the book to any significant degree (McCarthy in Rourke and McCarthy 2009). It's a conformism to the kind of remit prescribed by corporate market research that is especially visible in the architecture and materiality of McCarthy's novels as solid, tangible objects: their metadata, paratextual mediation, paper, binding, design, layout, use of white spaces, locations where the pages are cut and so on. Consider Marc Saporta's *Composition No.1* (1962), an experimental work made up of 150 unbound pages printed on one side only that can be read in any order and that influenced B.S. Johnson's own book-in-a-box, *The Unfortunates* (1969); or Jonathan Safran Foer's *Tree of Codes* (2010), which uses holes cut into Bruno Schulz's *Street of Crocodiles* (1934) to make a new text from an old one; or Kathy Acker's *Blood and Guts in High School* (1984), where the already unstable narrative of the story is further interrupted with pornographic drawings and poems; or Adam Thirlwell's (Haberdashers' Aske's Boys' School and Oxford) *Kapow!* (2012), which inserts blocks of text that are laid out visually in geometrical patterns into the narrative; or even Ali Smith's *How To Be Both* (2015), bound as it is in two versions in which either of its constitute parts (both labelled 'one') can be arranged in front of the other. By comparison novels such as *Men in Space* and *Satin Island* are really quite orthodox. Like the majority of books, they consist of numbered pages, laid out facing each other so as to mirror the two eyes of the human, thus rendering them easily navigable for a being with two hands and arms. Like the majority of books, these pages (which are free from holes, crossings out and other experiments with layout, font and typographical composition) are organised in a coherent, fixed, linear sequence to form a written narrative that is to be read in a progressive, temporal order. Like the majority of books, they are published professionally on a mass-industrial basis as authoritative, stable and uniform artefacts in the shape of print-on-paper codices. And, like the majority of books, they are marketed and distributed through the commercial book trade as consumer products.

I am not denying McCarthy's work, with its avant-garde influences, including its revision of the intermedial remixes of Burroughs and the recombination of fragments taken from a host of information media (literature, poetry, newspapers, cinema, radio), has the potential to upset England's cultural order as it currently stands. *Remainder* 'might be about two questions', Wark writes in her preface to the new edition of the novel published in 2015: 'Who gets to create? And when something is created, what remains?' (Wark 2015, vii). To which, having read McCarthy, we can answer: it is mostly middle-class white men with the necessary time and money who get to create. And what remains as surplus when they do is a whole host of unaddressed

questions: about their bourgeois liberal humanist model of subjectivity and its many assumptions
regarding the author, originality and copyright; but
also about the material qualities and properties of their
creations and their relationship to them. Importantly,
then, McCarthy directs us to look at the remainder of
communications technology: all the leftover 'extra-
neous stuff' (McCarthy 2015a, 83) that needs to be cut
and 'carted away' (114) to make creation possible – and
impossible, he and I would both maintain. At the same
time McCarthy makes it clear that any attempt to deal
fully with, or even speak about and know, this 'surplus
matter' is bound to fail (82). 'Poor Naz', the unnamed
narrator of *Remainder* says of the facilitator employed
to help him stage his reenactments. 'He wanted everything perfect, neat, wanted all matter organized and
filed away so that it wasn't a mess. He had to learn too:
matter's what makes us alive – the bitty flow, the scar
tissue, signature of the world's very first disaster and
promissory note guaranteeing its last. Try to iron it out
at your peril' (272). Indeed, it is precisely the impossibil-
ity of ever grasping the leftover matter of creation that
McCarthy is interested in.

What I *am* saying is that McCarthy's aesthetic tactics (and I'm rewriting Wark's rewriting of Raymond
Williams now) nevertheless continue to implicitly
exclude communication and its remainder. To put it
bluntly, if McCarthy really wants to avoid reaffirm-
ing liberal culture (and proceeding further down a
path that has already been mapped out in advance, a

path that by his own admission can lead nowhere else but to the middle-brow commercial novel), he needs to take far more care with the material reality of his own communications technology and with the *matter* of the contingent information media – writing, the book and the literary novel – that he uses to generate signals, messages, connections.

Chapter 7

'He Wants to Be Authentic, Is All': Literature as Technological Prosthesis

Perhaps the closest McCarthy comes to what we might think of as an antihumanist or posthumanist appreciation of how the human self is embedded within media and mediation, is Serge's dream sequence at the end of *C*:

> [H]e falls straight back into a lucid dream, once more of insects – only this time, all the insects have combined into a single, giant one from whose perspective, and from within whose body, he surveys this new dream's landscape. In effect, he *is* the insect. His gangly, mutinous limbs have grown into long feelers that jab and scrape at the air. What's more, the air presents back to these feelers surfaces with which contact is to be made, ones that *solicit* contact: plates, sockets, holes. As parts of him alight on and plug into these, space itself starts to jolt and cackle into action, and Serge finds himself connected

to everywhere, to all imaginable places. Signals hurtle through the sky, through time, like particles or flecks of matter, visible and solid. Each of his feelers has now found its corresponding touch-point, and the overall shape formed by this coupling, its architecture, has become apparent: it's a giant, tentacular wireless set, an insect-radio mounted on a plinth or altar. Serge is the votary kneeling down before it, arms stretched out to touch it; he's also the set itself – he's *both*. (2010, 300-301)

What's interesting about this passage from a posthumanist perspective is just how multiple and enmeshed with the world Serge is. He is human, but he is non-human too in that he is an insect and also a material media object. Serge is all of these things in fact: a human 'votary' *and* an 'insect-radio' set 'connected to everywhere, to all imaginable places'. For the most part, though, McCarthy's approach is too dialectical to enable him to take on board anything like the full extent to which the history of media 'is always and automatically at play' in his own work and ideas, and thus *their* 'interruptedness', *their* 'disarticulation' (2012). (Zadie Smith is not too far off the mark in characterising McCarthy's *Remainder* as an 'extreme form of dialectical materialism' [Smith 2009].) The problematic nature of McCarthy's dialecticism – *and* his materialism – becomes readily apparent if his account of technology is set alongside that of a theorist he particularly admires and whose insights on writing he is often held to have incorporated: Jacques Derrida.

As we know from *Transmission and the Individual Remix*, literature for McCarthy is a question of transmitting and receiving instruments. It's a matter of media technology, in other words. And he follows Freud in perceiving technology as prosthesis. To this end he shows how, in *Civilization and Its Discontents*, Freud describes 'engines as mechanical muscles, telescopes and microscopes as synthetic upgrades of the eye, cameras and gramophones as material extensions of memory' (2012). In doing so, McCarthy portrays the human's prosthetic relation to technology – including media technology (cameras, telephones, tape recorders, etc.) – as one in which the subject also suffers a disfigurement or demotion as a result of its interaction with the nonhuman tools it uses to communicate, this loss being something it can neither completely comprehend nor control nor eradicate. 'You'll find histories of loss ... lurking inside all media,' he writes. McCarthy thus operates within (and residually retains) the framework of a certain Western fantasy of becoming one with the materiality of the external world, and of communicating perfectly with others without the interruption, noise or opacity that are generated by mediation, even as he shows such perfection to be impossible. In the International Necronautical Society's 'Statement on Inauthenticity', for instance, McCarthy and Critchley make it clear that, as far as they are concerned, art is both the consequence and the 'experience of failed transcendence'.

What's more, it is a failure that is at the heart of both the General Secretary's novels and the Chief Philosopher's tomes. Here,

> Being is not full transcendence, the plenitude of the One or cosmic abundance, but rather an ellipsis, an absence, an incomprehensibly vast lack scattered with debris and detritus. Philosophy as the thinking of Being has to begin from the experience of disappointment that is at once religious (God is dead, the One is gone), epistemic (we know very little, almost nothing; all knowledge claims have to begin from the experience of limitation) and political (blood is being spilt in the streets as though it were champagne). (McCarthy and Critchley 2007, 4)

It is this desire for an idealised fullness of Being, a *we* without remainder, better, whole, complete, that motivates the naïve hero of *Remainder* to reenact moments of presence to avoid being awkward, artificial and 'second hand' like everyone else, including the media types he watches in Soho (McCarthy 2015a, 48). The death of a black man shot in the street in Brixton is one such moment. 'The truth is that, for me, this man had become a symbol of perfection. It may have been clumsy to fall from his bike, but in dying besides the bollards on the tarmac he'd done what I wanted to do: merged with the space around him, sunk and flowed into it until there was no distance between it and him ... He'd stopped being separate, removed, imperfect ... The spot that this had happened on was the ground zero of perfection

– all perfection: the one he'd achieved, the one I wanted, the one everyone else wanted but just didn't know they wanted' (177-178). As the hero's friend Gregg explains to the weird man known as the short councillor: '"He wants to be authentic, is all"' (206). Similarly in *C*, while all the other pilots and observers are afraid of the possibility of being shot down in flames, Serge is not. 'He's not unaware of it: just unbothered. The idea that his flesh could melt and fuse with the machine parts pleases him' (McCarthy 2010, 164).

Considering technology as prosthesis for McCarthy, then, means that

> we are promoted and demoted at the same time; augmented, but in diminished form. Technology might allow us to pass unpassable borders, penetrate and traverse impossible distances, to move even into and through the space reserved for gods – but this move also entails anxiety, bereavement. If you've got an artificial body part, it means you've lost an arm, a leg, that you're an amputee: like Orpheus, you've had your limbs ripped off.
>
> If technology in general is at once a form both of self-expression and of amputation, then the branch of it that concerns itself with information and its relay – communication technology – is a true field-hospital operating theatre floor of hacked-off limbs, of bereaved bodies. (2012)

Jacques Derrida, meanwhile, positions the prosthetic relation as the *technological condition*. The human, for him, cannot be dialectically opposed to nonhuman technology. It's not that there is an original, pre-existing subject that then comes into contact with an alien technology that somehow augments and diminishes this otherwise unified human self. It's that there is no real, natural, authentic human self to begin with. Technology, Derrida contends, 'has not simply added itself, from the outside or after the fact, as a foreign body. Or at least this foreign or dangerous supplement is "originarily" at work and in place in the supposedly ideal interiority of the "body and soul". It is indeed at the heart of the heart' (Derrida 1995, 244-245). To put it another way, technology is far from being merely an external tool that is used by the human for instrumental purposes – say, as mechanical muscles or material extensions of memory. (This is the classical Aristotelian view. Its flip side is the notion that technology has assumed power over its human creator. Consider the story of Frankenstein, or current anxieties around Silicon Valley and the threat its algorithmic systems of surveillance and behavioural control are taken to pose to privacy.) The human is also born out of its relation to technology. Adhering to the trajectory of Derrida's thought, what can now be perceived as the human's *originary* prosthetic relation to technology cannot be presented in a typical modernist fashion: say, in terms of a futurist extension (à la Marinetti's emphasis on speed), or a fall from a state of perfection and authenticity (and thus as loss, disappointment, bereavement, mourning). Indeed, whereas for McCarthy and the INS the answer to the question of how we deal with matter is *inauthentically* – something that rather intriguingly leads them to advance the concept of 'originary inauthenticity' (McCarthy and Critchley 2007, 10) – the human conceived in terms of the technological condition is neither authentic nor inauthentic, perfect nor imperfect, real nor fake. (Nor is it simply human *or* posthuman.) Technology is what makes the human *impossible*, to be sure. But it is also what makes the human *possible* in the first place. There is no human without technology. Still further, there is no human without communications technology. And if that seems a rather strange thing to say, consider how for many anthropologists what we know as the human only emerged with the use of tools, language especially, without which we are unable to communicate, or even think, in a particularly sophisticated manner.

Yet there's more. For while the self has always been technologically constituted, the human's prosthetic relation to technology is not always the same. The development of different communication technologies (e.g. language, writing, print), with their different material qualities and properties, has enabled different forms of this relation in different periods.[37] What the idea of *originary technicity* or *originary prostheticity* helps us to realise, then, is that when technology changes over time, so does the *nature* of its users and, with it, human thought and agency.[38] Technology thus escapes the control of its inventors to produce unforeseen possibilities, and with them a future – for both the human *and* technology – that is neither predictable nor programmable

(Hall 2002, 139-140). It is a realisation that is particularly significant for us today. Arguably, we are in the midst of a fourth great transformation in communications technology. If the first transformation was the development of speech and language, the second writing, and the third print (which was itself accompanied by other modes of analogue communication including radio, film and television), the fourth entails the shift from analogue to digital. In fact, it can be said that we are already living in the post-digital era, as the 'disruption brought upon by digital information technology has already occurred' (Cramer 2014, 17). Now, as we've seen, technology, in the guise of writing, the book, the school and so forth, has helped to produce the author as a liberal humanist subject. Which raises the question: what versions of the author function, what as yet unknown and unforeseeable transformations in human selfhood and philosophy, might twenty-first century technologies such as artificial intelligence and machine learning generate?

CHAPTER 8

Media Art and the Melancholy Impasse of the Anglo-American Novel

For all the influence of Derrida on his writing (and it's striking to be able to say this about an English novelist, given the general attitude toward theory), McCarthy is not prepared to engage rigorously with such questions. He devotes too little consideration to the materiality – the ink, paper, design, layout, typography, copyright licence and so on – of his own main medium of communication, the novel, and thus to all the 'messy, irksome matter' that is generally excluded from the understanding of literature (McCarthy 2015a, 17). Once again the problem with McCarthy's materialism is that, rather than rethinking the latter's relationship with idealism, he prefers to merely move from one side of the idealism/materialism dialectic to the other. As the INS put it:

> If form is perfect, if it is perfection itself, then how does one explain the obvious imperfection of the world, for the world is not perfect *n'est-ce*

pas? This is where matter – our undoing – enters into the picture. For the Greeks, the principle of imperfection was matter, *hyle*. Matter was the source of the corruption of form, of the corruption of the visible world. [...]

For us – necronauts, modern lovers of debris, radio and jetstreams – things are *precisely* the other way round: what is most real for us is not form, or God, but matter, the brute materiality of the external world. [...]

In short, against idealism in philosophy and idealist or transcendent conceptions of art, of art as pure and perfect form, we set a doctrine of poetic or necronautical materialism [...]. (McCarthy and Critchley 2007, 5-8)

Two issues emerge from this shift from idealism to materialism. The first concerns the importance McCarthy and the INS attach to letting 'things thing' and 'matter matter'. I'm détourning his words more and more now (along with those of some of his chief co-authors and interlocutors), but to what extent *does* McCarthy actually succeed in letting the 'orange orange and the flower flower' by making 'form as formless as possible' (McCarthy and Critchley 2007, 7)? Does McCarthy himself not 'extinguish matter and elevate it into form' (7), by trying to 'ingest all of reality into a system of thought' such as that concerning comedy, death and passivity that is articulated in the 'INS Statement on Inauthenticity' and enacted in his prose fiction (6)? Granted, it can be argued that the elevation of matter into form is inevitable to a certain degree; that we can never just let matter matter. The important thing, according to McCarthy and the INS, is to be aware of this, to realise it is ultimately impossible, and to refuse to evade the futility of the task by resorting to fantasies of authenticity including that represented by the unified autonomous subject. Dreams of this nature should be abandoned. 'Any attempt at authenticity slips back into an inauthenticity from which it cannot escape, but which it would like to evade' (10). This is why McCarthy and the INS claim we need to deal with matter inauthentically, while simultaneously remaining self-consciously aware of our inauthenticity (a splitting of the subject in two that is different from being authentic). Yet, as we know, far from being split, the authorial self that McCarthy performs with his novels is often more of a 'complete, godlike even ... heroic subject' (McCarthy and Critchley 2007, 9).[39]

The second issue that arises out of his switch from one side of the idealism/materialism dichotomy to the other concerns less the degree to which McCarthy *is* or *is not* able to mutter and utter the mattering of matter. It's more that in the process of 'trying (and failing) to speak about the thing itself and not just ideas about the thing', he extinguishes the intractable matter of his own novels (McCarthy and Critchley 2007, 7). He neglects to deal with the stain of *their* materiality, that messy remainder or trace, and the associated 'reality of industry' (McCarthy and Critchley 2007, 8; see also McCarthy

2007). Instead, there is a 'movement of evasion' here as well, one that serves ultimately to reveal McCarthy's own 'embeddedness in materiality' (McCarthy and Critchley, 10). In remixing, for example, he may be recombining fragments taken from old, contemporary and futural media. Yet he does not leave their 'fragmentary, collated character' unmasked (McCarthy 2012). McCarthy wants to make an intervention by having his work read in a crowded media environment in which it is competing for attention with a host of other signals and transmissions. So he gathers his fragments together and merges them into the conventional material configuration of the novel – something that is not interrogated but is rather accepted as the natural form for a (quasi-modernist) literary writer to adopt.

Ironically, it's McCarthy's very materialism that leads him to take insufficient notice of the way in which the brute physical qualities and properties of books as media-technological objects have an active bearing both on the ideas they convey and on our constitution as diehard bourgeois liberal humanist subjects. He may regard the literary novel as a privileged medium for remixing certain antihumanist ideas in order to be relatively critical of liberal society and its emphasis on the human individual. (For Hayles, the narrator in *Remainder* provides a nightmarish vision of what happens when actions are undertaken 'without the connections created by embeddedness in the world' [Hayles 2017, 89].) But as *Remainder, Men in Space, C et al.* testify, as far as McCarthy is concerned, the novel is not a medium for self-consciously taking on board the implications of contemporary antihumanist or posthumanist theory for his own identity as an author. This includes the notion that our agency and consciousness emerges out of the relational intra-actions of a heterogeneous assemblage of humans, technologies and other actors and elements.[40] Nor is the literary novel a medium for performatively exploring how agency and consciousness may be changing as a result of those transformations currently taking place in the concrete form and materiality of the media technologies with which we communicate. Above all, the novel is not a medium in which to experiment with reinventing how culture and ideas are *physically* created, circulated and communicated, on the basis that we may indeed be entering into a new landscape (albeit in an overlapping, zig-zagging fashion that is neither linear nor progressive). It is a landscape that is more than post-digital: it is post-Gutenberg too. But McCarthy does not want to take things that far. He is clearly reluctant to carry the 'literary work itself beyond all boundaries, not least the very ones that gave rise to it in the first place' (2012).

It is precisely out of an ambition to take the literary work beyond its current confines that many writers *have* turned to art and to the kind of experiments with form that are enabled by digital media. (Mark Amerika was a remix pioneer in this respect with 1997's GRAMMATRON and 1999's PHON:E:ME.)[41] As far as his prose fiction is concerned, however, McCarthy is wary of going down this media art route.[42] He prefers to take a path associated with Thomas Pynchon, Sheila Heti and others in the US. 'In the UK most of the literary talent has gone into the art world. Writing novels in a way that questions what the form might be, that seems to be happening more in New York than in London — Tao Lin, Sheila Heti, Ben Lerner, Ben Marcus. In America you have less of this curse of middle-brow. People either want to read real trash or Thomas Pynchon' (McCarthy in Kachka 2012).[43] While taking the latter path of writing novels in order to question what the novel might be is perfectly understandable for tactical, Trojan Horse reasons, the problem remains: without explicitly and rigorously acknowledging the novel, its form and materiality, as his chosen broadcast technology, without dislocating, troubling or at least rerouting this circuit, his work does indeed collapse 'into the reverb of communication', as Wark characterises the undoing of modernism, 'lost in the noise of the commodity and the spectacle' (Wark 2015, x). McCarthy may disarticulate and then rearticulate what it is to be an author and to write novels. As a reminder, it's to send transmissions out and bring them back together again, gathered from a wide range of information media, both new and old, in remixed form. Yet it's noticeable that for the political theorist Chantal Mouffe there is a messy point in-between the process of disarticulation and rearticulation where common-sense ways of being are radically transformed by artists in order to construct 'new practices and new subjectivities', and thus 'help subvert the existing configuration of power' (2013, 105). ('One

of the foremost tasks of art has always been the creation of a demand which could be fully satisfied only
later', Walter Benjamin writes in a similar vein [1973,
239].) Significantly, this crucial transformative aspect
is for the most part missing from McCarthy's literary
work. The author and novel may be lifted out of the general flow of information media from time to time. (On
occasion McCarthy has described this suspension as
a productive moment of pause or interruption. Rather
than representing a lack or emptiness, it's a moment
that constitutes a generative space, a buffer zone, a
recess, in which something else can potentially emerge
out of the remainder, even if that 'something else' does
get recuperated eventually.) However, the author and
the novel are not returned to this flow in a different
(material) reconfiguration, metamorphosed, otherwise.
Instead, their pre-existing natural form – that of the
grand individual (male) genius and print-on-paper book
of McCarthy's canonical modernist heroes – remains
more or less the same. 'I'm just doing what the novel
should do', McCarthy says, 'and trying to achieve the
things the novels I most admire achieved' (McCarthy in
Rourke and McCarthy 2009).

There is a blockage, then. As Dr Filip tells Serge in C:
'Jam, block, stuck. Instead of transformation, only repetition. Need to free what's blocking, break whole rhythm
of intoxication – then good transformation can resume
and things will pass through you and make you open up.
You still are only adolescent: still have much transformation to perform' (2010, 105). The trouble is McCarthy

does not regard mutating the habitual performance of the unified, autarkic, autonomous author and of the second-hand technological prosthesis of the book (to name just a couple of his blind spots) as a means of opening things up to a transformed, antihumanist mode of subjectivity and creativity. He associates any such break with the exhausted system of liberal humanism and its values too much with amputation, dissolution and death. As the narrator of *Satin Island* remarks about the skydiver with the severed parachute and how the whole fabric of that system (consisting of his instructor, his equipment, those packing his rig, the laws of physics and so on) had come apart: 'That, and not his death, was the catastrophe that had befallen him. We're all going to die: there's nothing so disastrous about that, nothing in its ineluctability that undermines the structure of our being. But for the faith, the blind, absolute faith into whose arms he had entrusted his existence, from whose mouth he'd sought a widespread affirmation of its very possibility – for that to suddenly be plucked away: that must have been atrocious' (McCarthy 2015b, 98). McCarthy's residual mourning over the futility of perfection and authenticity, of the human fusing with the nonhuman world, thus remains unresolved, jammed, stuck, in spite of his extensive reading of Freud. And it's because he doesn't quite appreciate this is the case (or is it because, at some level, he doesn't want to appreciate it is the case, due to the *atrocious* implications of doing so?) that McCarthy is unable to move beyond the model of both the pre-formatted, bourgeois liberal humanist literary writer and that of the commercial codex book. His is very much a failed transcendence in this respect. Hence we get the 'melancholy impasse' out of which the Anglo-American novel still has to work its way, melancholy being precisely an unresolved mourning for Freud (McCarthy 2011a; Freud 1917). Moreover, 'whatever is suppressed repeats', as Freud also teaches us (McCarthy 2006). Does this lesson of Freud's explain why McCarthy reenacts the experience of failed transcendence and unresolved mourning again and again in his novels, in a loop, endlessly? '"End this" – or perhaps, conversely, "Endless" …' (McCarthy 2010, 179).

Of course, it can be argued – as Wark and others certainly do – that McCarthy's work does not in fact 'claim to be doing anything new': that it self-consciously and semi-fictitiously 'imitates the once new, now old, methods of Modernism', just as the activities of the INS playfully imitate those of the Surrealists, Futurists and Situationists. 'It is about – and indeed maybe it is – the remainder, the reverb, the noise of communication, rather than the act of communication or even mimesis. It is about the leftover trash heap of aesthetic strategies' (Wark 2015, x). Viewed from this perspective, instead of farcically pretending to create something *new* that would establish him as a God or master of creation, McCarthy's 'response to the materiality of our inauthentic state is a more passive and less heroic decision' (McCarthy and Critchley 2007, 11). It is about seeing himself from outside and laughingly reenacting the role of the (modernist) literary author and novelist, or what remains of it, out of all the surplus matter, debris, detritus, dirt, junk, mess and waste of creation. Accordingly, he refuses to endeavour to move beyond the tradition of bourgeois liberal humanism by inventing different *dispositifs*, as Foucault would have it (Foucault, 1980). McCarthy accepts that the author cannot resolve the impasse in which the novel currently finds itself. And he gets a 'strangely melancholy joy' from recognising this and from repeatedly writing comedic books of fiction about it (2012).

He even goes so far as to position such repetition with difference as being 'counterintuitive to a humanist or even a contemporary middle-brow literary credo where you're meant to be unique', whereas in fact it's 'very much like Warhol: the boringness of just repeating the same with difference is much more interesting' (McCarthy 2016, 64). At the end of *Remainder* the narrator puts it like this: '"Just keep on. The same pattern. It will all be fine"' (275). The problem is, though, it isn't fine. As was the case with the *good* remixers we looked at earlier, by adopting the logic of secondariness in a universe that has no origin, and carrying that logic to its most extreme configuration, McCarthy (*very much like Warhol*) is able to achieve a kind of primacy within this universe nonetheless. He may contend that there is no original creation, just 'repetition, repetition and repetition' (McCarthy in Rourke and McCarthy 2009). Yet his repetitions are *different but the same* (certainly more than they are *the same but different*). While each repetition inevitably introduces a certain degree of difference, there is little or no transformation in his unmaking and remaking of literariness, of what it is to be an author and to compose novels. No interruption or rupture. No event '(*events!* if you want those, you'd best stop reading now)' (2015b).[44] Consequently, McCarthy's modulated reenactment of the modernist writer continues to function within the literary economy to all intents and purposes *as if* it is a grand, inspired, solitary genius, much like his heroes Burroughs, Beckett and Ballard (The Leys School and Cambridge) – and Blanchot and Barthes for that matter. (What is more, this is the case even though, as McCarthy says himself of middle-brow fiction, 'endlessly recycling' these kinds of 'tired humanist clichés under the guise of originality, is in truth profoundly unoriginal' [2017, 269].) His replaying of the death and afterlife of modernism in novels such as *C* and *Satin Island* is thus held as creating new meaning, and is understood, culturally and legally, very much as an original authorial act on his part. And his work is validated accordingly by critics, prize committees and the organisers of academic conferences, all of whom have little difficulty in ascribing an 'official' literary authorship and artistic agency to him as a person, bestowing on his writing the 'seal of "legitimacy"' in the process (2006).[45] One cannot help wonder, then, just how much *does* McCarthy disrupt liberal society's contemporary cult of the individual?

A Stubborn Fury

In conclusion, we can see that in order to *do what needs to be done* McCarthy does not allow his engagement with theory and the avant-garde to cause too much trouble for the parameters of what is permissible, certainly as the English cultural establishment set them. His literary antihumanism and modernism may have the potential to subvert the existing configurations of power and privilege. Yet McCarthy employs both to reenact and reaffirm rather than to unsettle those normative, bourgeois, liberal humanist ways of being and doing that one needs to conform to if one wants to be taken seriously as a writer of novels and well-crafted articles for periodicals such as *The London Review of Books.*

Eribon and Louis have something of an advantage over McCarthy in this regard. Their non-normative backgrounds (if we want to stay with the contingent framework of the biographical author) mean that the morals and habits imposed on them by polite bourgeois society don't matter nearly so much. Growing up gay, poor and working class in northern France, Eribon and Louis were constantly reminded that they weren't 'normal', that they were 'breaking the rules' (Eribon 2013, 199). Consequently, they have fewer qualms about confronting the expectations of the established order – and this includes some of society's manufactured values and hierarchies regarding what constitutes a *good* piece of writing. As Louis puts it in *Who Killed My Father?*, the third of his memoirs to be translated into English: 'I am not afraid of repeating myself because what I am writing, what I am saying, does not answer to the standards of literature, but to those of necessity and desperation, to standards of fire' (Louis 2019b, 14).

The situation also leads Eribon to recognise 'a kind of blown-up image' of what he himself went through in Pierre Bourdieu's account of his own years as an adolescent youth from humble origins (160). In *Sketch for a Self-Analysis*, Eribon finds 'obvious traces' of Bourdieu's '"clashes with school discipline"', '(difficult) personal character' and general 'social ineptitude' in the way he later conducted his intellectual life (Eribon 2013, 160-61; quoting Bourdieu 2007, 94). Such signs are particularly visible in Bourdieu's 'evident lack of respect for the rules of bourgeois decorum that reign in university circles and tend to impose themselves on anyone who does not wish to be excluded from the "scholarly community", rules that insist that people follow established norms regarding "intellectual debate" when what is at stake clearly has to do with a political struggle' (Eribon 2013, 161). It is a 'rebellion – a "stubborn fury" – that continued in and through the production of knowledge', Eribon notes approvingly (162; quoting Bourdieu,

96). (It's no coincidence that, in addition to writing his memoirs on working-class life, Louis has edited a book on the work of Bourdieu [2013].)

Observing that their non-normative backgrounds mean Eribon and Louis have fewer qualms about confronting the expectations of the established order is not to overlook the fact that they encounter many of the same problems as McCarthy, even if those problems are played out somewhat differently in their work. When it comes to the material practicalities of publishing, for instance, rather than rebelling, Eribon and Louis respect much of the scaffolding of bourgeois decorum and its '"stable points of reference"' (Eribon 2013, 72). To reappropriate McCarthy one last time, consider the way in which, with *Returning to Reims, The End of Eddy, History of Violence* and now *Who Killed My Father?*, they are 'operating with materials and within frames' – of the biographical human individual, the work, the book, the proper name, intellectual property and so on – 'that are neither of [their] own making, nor politically neutral', but are assumed and accepted as given nonetheless (McCarthy 2017, 268-269). Where is the critical thought, the political struggle, the stubborn fury with regard to these datum points? For all their emphasis on rebelling in and through the technologies of knowledge production, where is the endeavour to say and do 'anything other than what's been agreed upon' here (de Lagasnerie and Louis 2015)? In fact, just as McCarthy's respect for those frames and formats that are associated with the literary novel means *C* and *Satin Island* can ultimately be put up for the likes of the Man Booker Prize, is it precisely because Eribon and Louis *do* play by many of the immanent rules of intellectual debate, and *do not* actually create difficulties for our ideas of the author, originality, copyright and so forth, that their otherwise disrespectfully critical books can be taken seriously by the bourgeois establishment in Europe and beyond, and they themselves held up as charismatic *celebrity* theorists?

Nevertheless, what is so inspiring about their work, at least for me, is their willingness to go that bit further than McCarthy when it comes to actually questioning the norms and prejudices of white, masculinist, middle-class, liberal humanist culture. That, and the openness they display in doing so toward promoting heterodoxy and critical thought with regard to theory and what it is currently considered to be too. This is the reason I wanted to frame my reading of how writing works in elitist Britain with Eribon and Louis, regardless of the importance they attach to the absolutely authentic auto-biographical self (an emphasis that, with McCarthy's help, we can see is less opposed to the neoliberal project than they would like to believe). I wanted to both begin and end with them because I *do* think theory needs to be reinvented, due to the fact *it is* so bourgeois, liberal and humanist in its habits.

But I also wanted to do so to show what is at stake in the kinds of questions I am raising here and why they really matter. For, thanks to Eribon and Louis (*and to McCarthy as well*) we can appreciate that a lot more than simply reading French theory in larger numbers will be needed to foster a culture in England that is *not* so liberal, humanist and anti-intellectual. Publishing fewer texts by people who went to private school or Oxbridge, and more by writers from other, less privileged socioeconomic backgrounds, will not be sufficient either – nor will generating greater opportunities for people from other social settings to attend these institutions.

Various methods of achieving the latter have been proposed in recent years. Andrew Adonis (Kingham Hill School and Oxford), the Labour peer and former education minister, advocates the establishment of new Oxbridge colleges for the disadvantaged. Others demand the introduction of legislation to ensure limits are placed on the number of private school pupils entering Oxbridge; and that Russell Group universities (which include Oxford and Cambridge) distribute undergraduate places according to the percentage of the general population that is educated by the state (which would currently mean only 7% of their intake would have attended a private school).[46] Still others go so far as to support the allocation of secondary school places by lottery and the gifting of vouchers to disadvantaged parents to pay for the private education of their children (Goldthorpe, quoted in Wilby 2020). Any of all of these would be a start – and an extremely meaningful one at that. As, indeed, is the funding of a number of #Merky Cambridge University scholarships by the rapper Stormzy. (This initiative has led to a significant increase in the number of black students applying to study there.) The problem with most such ideas, however – as with that of social mobility in general – is they tend to leave the status quo intact. More people from a wider variety of places and backgrounds may get to publish and tell their stories. Yet it does not follow that widening participation will necessarily lead to a greater diversity of perspectives and practices. Moreover these 'different' people are sent to the same, pre-existing, 'good' institutions, with the result that the wider structures involved in the maintenance of social injustice remain unchanged.[47] Indeed, as far as their ways of being and doing are concerned, these different (i.e. 'better') people may actually strive to defend and reinforce the current structures of privilege and power, precisely because their victories have been so hard won. (Is this one of the reasons why those who have been able to climb the social ladder tend to place so much store by their own backstories?)

What we learn from a careful reading of Eribon, Louis and McCarthy is that it's not only *which* subjects get to contribute to English culture by writing and publishing that is crucial, it's *how* those subjects write and publish. It's not even just how writing, publishing and subjectivity are conceived that matters, it's also how they are actually *performed*. Of course it is incredibly important to have more women, BAME, working-class, radically queer, neuroatypical and differently abled people (as well as those at the intersections of these different identities) communicating from their specific locations, whatever those locations may be and however they may be understood. Just as important, though, is that they and others do so in ways that are more than simply iterations of the prevailing bourgeois liberal humanism and its many assumptions regarding how culture is created and disseminated. In other words, if, in the future, we *do* want to develop an appreciation of life, agency and subjectivity that is more complex and diverse, then we need to reinvent *how* we work, think and act too.

Notes

1   Unless indicated otherwise, all further references in the text
    are to the US version of *Returning to Reims* (2013). Some mate-
    rial from Part I of *A Stubborn Fury* first appeared in Hall (2019).

2   Put very crudely, if antihumanism is concerned with decen-
    tring humanism and the human from their traditional place
    at the heart of Western thought, posthumanism is concerned
    with doing so by undermining the boundary that separates
    the human from the nonhuman, be it animals, insects, objects
    or technologies.

3   I perhaps owe the reader an explanation as to why I have cho-
    sen *How Writing Works in Elitist Britain* as the subtitle for this
    book rather than *How Writing Works in Elitist England*. As I not-
    ed in the preface, my subtitle is derived from the 2019 Sutton
    Trust report, *Elitist Britain*. And, to be sure, the kind of debates
    over privilege, inequality and exclusiveness that I am engag-
    ing with in this book are often conducted in terms of Britain
    or the UK rather than England. At the same time, I've tried
    to avoid writing about the cultures of the three nations that
    make up Great Britain as if they were more or less the same
    (an easy thing to do given that of England dominates the oth-
    ers so much). Indeed, the reason my main concern here is with
    how writing works in England is because the relation between
    class and social mobility takes a different shape in each of
    these countries, with much of the discussion over anti-intel-
    lectualism and educational uniformity in British culture be-
    ing rooted in what are largely English factors.
    	This focus on how writing works in elitist England is also
    why I don't go on to provide comparable figures regarding the
    unequal distribution of opportunities for those from different

backgrounds in France. For one historical comparison of the
divergent attitudes toward the intellectual in England and
France, see Jeremy Jennings, 'Deaths of the Intellectual: A
Comparative Autopsy'. Among the contrasts that Jennings
locates between the two traditions the following is especially
worth highlighting: 'From Zola onwards, if not from before,
the French intellectual has defined the identity of France
in terms of universal ideals of truth, justice, and the rights
of man and has chosen to locate their physical embodiment
in the institutions of the Republic, one and indivisible. In
England, a distrust of abstract ideas combined with a delight
in particularity focused patriotic nostalgia upon the peoples,
places, and architecture of a much-revered English landscape'
(2002: 121). Think Melvyn Bragg (Oxford) and his *Cumbrian
Trilogy* of *The Hired Man* (1969), *A Place in England* (1970) and
Kingdom Come (1980); or, to offer a more recent example, Simon
Armitage and his *Magnetic Field: The Marsden Poems* (2020).

Jennings also makes the point that the relative weakness
and deficiency of the French university system means that it
'might crush its participants but it does not always, as elsewhere, domesticate and compromise them' (2002, 124). In
other words, the education system in France does not bring
writers under the control of what, according to Jennings, is
its own prevailing 'anti-intellectualism', in quite the manner that, as we'll see, a public school and Oxbridge education
do with regard to those in England (123). Couple this to what
he identifies as the 'failure of liberalism ever to develop deep
roots in French political culture' (126), and it becomes easier to
understand why it was France and not England that saw the
emergence of the radical, abstract, humanist philosophy of
Jean-Paul Sartre, followed shortly afterwards by the antihumanist variant of Foucault and others.

4   For a different reading of this English literary generation, see
Sarah Brouillette's *Literature and the Creative Economy* (2014).
According to Brouillette, rather than European modernism
it is the realist novels of Ian McEwan, Kazuo Ishiguro *et al.*
that may actually be the more radical today. The latter writers
know very well that their critiques of neoliberal capitalism
are ineffective: that as authors they are incorporated and in-
strumentalised at the same time as they are trying to remain
autonomous. Brouillette sees McEwan, *et al.* as 'hesitatingly

qualifying traditional ideologies of authorship from within the tradition itself', nevertheless. Their writings denote, for her, 'not a contended giving up of one's controlling position for the sake of fostering a participatory community of creators but rather a struggle against oneself, against one's own work, and against the traditions of one's medium' (16).

5   Waidner raises the intriguing question of why the majority of 'politically acute avant-garde writers' in the UK are today coming through film, art, poetry and performance, as opposed to prose literature. By way of response, Waidner compares the situation of queer avant-garde fiction to that of the other arts. Although queer and experimental film, art, poetry and performance remain marginal, they were all able to emerge and survive thanks to funding in the early 1980s from institutions such as the Greater London Council (GLC) and the newly founded public service broadcaster Channel 4. In fact, they have positively thrived in the case of queer and trans avant-garde performance. By contrast, there is 'hardly any queer avant-garde fiction', Waidner claims. 'Neither has there been a significant tradition' of such writing (2018, 15).

6   Solomon is here referring to research by Reeves and Friedman (2017).

7   That said, the figures for 2018 do show an improvement on those for 2017 when, of 9,115 children's books published in the UK, only 4% featured BAME characters. Just 1% had a BAME lead character in 2017 and 96% had no BAME characters whatsoever (Centre for Literacy in Primary Education 2018). I have used BAME here and throughout as it is the terminology adopted by such reports. However, I want to acknowledge some consider 'black, Asian and minority ethnic' too generalizing as a descriptor and thus as unhelpful, not least because different minority groups experience racism differently. See, for example, 'A Statement on Eradicating the Use of the Term BAME' by Coventry's Belgrade Theatre (2020). Some now prefer the term Black and Global Majority because of its shift in emphasis from minority to majority; others Indigenous Peoples and People of Color (IPOC).

8   Staying with publishing a moment longer, anti-racist books such as Reni Eddo-Lodge's *Why I'm No Longer Talking to White*

People About Race (2017) and Akala's *Natives: Race and Class in the Ruins of Empire* (2018) headed the bestseller lists in Britain in the wake of the Black Lives Matter protests that took place after the death in US police custody of George Floyd in May 2020. Indeed, Eddo-Lodge became the first black Briton ever to top both the non-fiction paperback and overall UK book charts during this period, while Bernadine Evaristo became the first woman of colour to top that for paperback fiction with her novel, *Girl, Woman, Other* (2019). The question is: will these developments lead to longer-term changes to an industry in which only 13% of respondents to a 2019 Publishers Association survey identified as BAME (Publishers Association 2020a)? The same survey found 'more than a quarter of respondents growing up in the South East of England (26.1%), with a further 13.9% growing up in the East of England, and 11.2% growing up in London. The North East of England had the lowest representation of all of the English regions, with just 1.2% of respondents. The South West (6.8%), West Midlands (5.0%), North West (4.4%), Yorkshire and the Humber (4.4%), and East Midlands (3.5%), all had significantly lower responses than the South East, East and London. Northern Ireland (0.8%), Scotland (2.5%), Wales (1.7%) and Ireland (1.3%) accounted for just 6.3% combined' (Publishers Association 2020b, 17-18). Even if there are changes to the publishing industry, what will the nature of those changes be? As will become clear over the course of what follows, my concern is that when it comes to how literature is created, published and disseminated, the result is likely to be different but more or less the same. To paraphrase Eddo-Lodge, injustice will thrive, but there will be more women and people of colour at the head of it.

9   In *Elitist Britain* (2019) the Sutton Trust provides related figures for important broadcasters and editors in news media ('43% having been privately educated and 36% graduating from Oxbridge') and newspaper columnists ('44% attending either Oxford or Cambridge, with 44% also attending independent school, with a third coming through the 'independent school to Oxbridge "pipeline" alone').

10   For more on some of the other professions I mentioned – pol-
     itics, medicine, the civil service and so on – see Kirby (2016)
     and the Sutton Trust (2019).

11   Research has shown that the pandemic has had a dispropor-
     tionate impact on BAME communities when it comes to who
     has been critically ill with the virus, with black people be-
     ing four times more likely to die in England and Wales than
     white people, according to the Office of National Statistics
     (ONS 2020a; #CharitySoWhite 2020), and men in low-skilled
     manual occupations nearly four times more likely to die than
     professionals (ONS 2020b). It is also by far those in low-paid
     jobs, along with female workers and the young, who are go-
     ing to be hit hardest in the future. This is due to the closure
     of sectors such as arts, retail and leisure services during the
     first lockdown, and the fact children in the most deprived
     schools were able to spend considerably less time learning at
     home over this period than their privately educated counter-
     parts, more than a third being without access to the internet
     or an electronic device such as a laptop or phone (Joyce and
     Xu 2020; Cullinane and Montacute 2020). It's important to be
     aware in this context that black students are almost twice as
     likely to be in receipt of free schools meals as white students,
     the figures being approximately 20% to 11% respectively.

12   By contrast (and to show just how narrow and ingrained the
     worldview of middle-class white men can be), McCarthy re-
     calls in *Typewriters, Bombs, Jellyfish* how, when the Serpentine
     Gallery asked him whether he would like to conduct a public
     dialogue with someone as part of a marathon of poetry they
     were putting on, he rejected their rather stock idea it should
     be with 'some Faber-and-Faber versifier or other'. His idea
     of suggesting someone different in this context, however,
     turns out to be the cricket commentator Henry Blofeld – 'who
     received a top-drawer classical education at Eton ... and
     Cambridge', McCarthy feels it necessary to add (2017, 219-220).

13   After the 2011 jury for the Man Booker Prize stated that
     they were going to privilege writing that was 'readable', the
     Goldsmiths Prize was established in 2013 – with Josipovici
     as one of the judges – explicitly to encourage experiments de-
     signed to open 'up new possibilities for the novel form'. For
     an analysis of the Goldsmiths Prize, and especially of how a

competition 'launched to counter the Man Booker's privileging of readability over formal audacity' has found itself having to 'try hard to assert the accessibility and entertaining qualities' of its winners nevertheless, see Drąg (2019, 52).

It is certainly noticeable that the Goldsmiths Prize literary experiments – from Eimear McBride's *A Girl Is a Half-Formed Thing* (2013), the first winner, through to Lucy Ellmann's *Ducks, Newburyport* (2019), the winner in 2019 – take quite a conventional material form. Regardless of any formal experimentation on their part, be it in terms of linguistic ingenuity, generic hybridity or an interweaving of multiple voices, they are still immediately recognisable as print-on-paper codex novels and books. It is also interesting that such *experiments* have become relatively acceptable only now, when a format has been found through which they can be commodified, marketed, branded and promoted fairly easily: namely, a contest whereby individual authors and texts are forced to compete against each other in order to gain advantage in the struggle for financial support, book contracts, creative writing posts, recognition and attention. Prizes such as the Goldsmiths can thus be said to promote and indeed help shape a particular form of subjectivity: that of the rational, competitive, self-interested individual of late capitalism.

It seems significant, then, that outside of the Goldsmiths a number of winning writers and artists have begun to push back against this ethos by insisting on sharing their prize with the other shortlisted 'competitors' or nominees. The artist Theaster Gates shared the Artes Mundi prize in 2015, for instance, as did Helen Martin (Oxford) with both the 2016 Turner prize and Hepworth sculpture prize, and the author Olivia Laing when she won the 2019 James Tait Black award. More recently still, all four artists shortlisted for the 2019 Turner prize – Lawrence Abu Hamdan, Helen Cammock, Oscar Murillo and Tai Shani – declared themselves a collective in the name of 'commonality, multiplicity and solidarity', and so were declared joint winners.

14   Other sections of British society are not necessarily any better in this respect. As the rapper and author Darren McGarvey notes of the working-class community in which he grew up in Scotland: 'The act of reading, and indeed all forms of academic achievement, were regarded by many of my male peers

as either feminine or the preserve of posh people and freaks' (McGarvey 2018, xxiii).

15   For a recent, self-confessed 'moderate' discussion of the inequality generated by Britain's education system, see Francis Green (Oxford) and David Kynaston (Wellington College and Oxford), *Engines of Privilege* (2019).

16   Similarly, as a public broadcaster the BBC is supposed to be politically neutral. Yet when the grammar school-educated John Humphrys retired in September 2019, the only regular presenter on either the BBC's Today or Newsnight programmes who was not educated privately was Emily Maitlis (Cambridge). The political bias inherent in such a situation is rarely acknowledged, however. And this is the case even though much of the country's appreciation of politics is shaped by the upper-middle-class voices found on these programmes, who nearly all have the same political agenda – even though they don't think of it as an agenda, just objective reporting and polite common sense.

17   One of the latest manifestations of this backlash is the idea that the academic left, in the form of postmodernists, poststructuralists and deconstructionists, is in part to blame for the rise of the 'post-truth' politics characteristic of the era of Donald Trump and Boris Johnson. I don't want to spend too much time on this idea, representing as it does a blatant misunderstanding of antihumanist theory. Suffice it to say, so-called poststructuralist or deconstructionist theory was never about saying there is no such thing as truth – nor indeed the human. And even if it had been, theory has never had the kind of power needed to get such conceptions commonly accepted and acted upon.

18   A recent variation on this defamation theme can be found in a UK political context with the infamous 'Weirdos and Misfits' blog and recruitment ad of Boris Johnson's chief adviser, Dominic Cummings (Durham School and Oxford), and its rejection of 'Oxbridge English graduates who chat about Lacan at dinner parties' (i.e. abstract ideas concerning language, interpretation and critique rather than more concrete subjects such as the computer modeling and super-forecasting that is made possible by big data and artificial intelligence) (2020).

For more on the libertarian neoliberalism of the Johnson government (which has also been labelled 'authoritarian entre-
preneurialism'), see my 'Postdigital Politics' (forthcoming).

19   Here I'm remixing the language of Mark Amerika from *remixthecontext* (2018, 90).

20   The word 'datum' means a proposition that is assumed, given
or taken for granted, upon which a theoretical framework can
be constructed or a conclusion drawn as a result of reasoning or calculation. In engineering the datum point is the place
from which measurements are taken. The datum point itself,
however, is not checked or questioned. As the position from
which measurements are made it is precisely *a given* (see Hall
2016, 47; Hall 2017).

21   According to Nielson Book Research, sales of memoirs in the
UK increased by 42% in the twelve months leading to May
2019, in part fuelled by the popularity of books written by
real people in *real* jobs (doctors, nurses, teachers), as opposed
to the celebrity authors previously seen as driving book sales:
i.e. Adam Kay (*This Is Going To Hurt*) and the Secret Barrister
rather than Sharon Osbourne and Peter Kay. Meanwhile,
the 2018 Authors Income Survey by the Authors Guild of US
professional writers, including those like Freeman who live
abroad, indicates that: 'Median incomes of all published authors who were surveyed ... for all writing-related activities
was $6,080, down 3% from four years ago. This is down from a
$10,500 median income in 2009 according the Authors Guild's
last survey.... Literary writers experienced the biggest decline
(down 27% in four years) in amount they earned from book-
related income' (Authors Guild 2019).

22   Although there is no space to do so here, it would be interesting to explore the extent to which autography contains
the basis for a renewal of literature. I am thinking of Eribon
and Louis' displacement of the distinctions between critical
theory and creative writing in their memoirs; and also of the
attempts to develop new, genre-defying literary forms such
as auto-fiction and auto-theory by the likes of Rachel Cusk
(Oxford) and Maggie Nelson respectively.

23   For more, see Lamont (1987). Working-class and ex-working-
class writers have of course been speaking about violence,

exploitation and repression for some time. What I find especially productive about the contributions of Eribon and Louis to this field is the importance they place both on using theory to do so and on reinventing theory in the process. In this respect their writing is distinct from a lot of working-class literature and the contemporary research on it, which, according to Nilsson and Lennon certainly, 'remains theoretically backward' (Nilsson and Lennon 2017). I am grateful to Bo Reimer for encouraging me to articulate this point.

24 Kit de Waal, the editor of *Common People: An Anthology of Working Class Writers* (2019), a book designed to discover new working-class voices, is quite explicit about this aspect of the contemporary memoir. 'The collection was originally planned to be mainly serious fiction', she says, 'but then the question arose: "How will we know if the voices are for real?". The decision was taken 'to ask for memoir, because you can't fake it so easily' (Adams 2019, 10).

25 The end of *Satin Island* provides another example. In *Recessional*, a book based on a talk he first gave in Zurich in 2014, McCarthy acknowledges that this ending is lifted 'straight from Balzac's *Le Père Goriot*' (2016, 57).

26 I'm building here on Geoffrey Bennington's reading of Jean-Jacques Rousseau, which is in turn building on the philosophy of Jacques Derrida. A similar undecidability is present in McCarthy's account of 'the contingency of "natural" processes of inheritance' in *Tintin and The Secret of Literature*: 'Look at the way Tintin acquires eventual possession of all three parchments in *The Secret of the Unicorn*: by taking Max Bird's wallet, which contains two of them, from the pickpocket who stole it and then getting Thompson and Thomson to bring him the third, again from Bird, when they arrest the antiques dealer. This is extremely dubious practice, to say the least. The "correct" procedure would be to return the two wallets to Bird, criminal or not, enter a claim for them and let justice run its course. But Tintin takes it and gets away with taking it, because Thompson and Thomson not only fail to intervene and stop him but also actively help him in his plundering. Justice is on his side; it works for him' (McCarthy 2006).

27   It is worth emphasizing that not all forms of piracy are in-
      herently opposed to capitalism. As I show in *Pirate Philosophy*,
      with their 'convictions about freedom, rights, duties, obliga-
      tions', certain enactments of piracy are actually fundamental
      to capitalism (2016, 139-140). See Mason (2008) and Allende
      (2018) for two entrepreneurial takes on piracy.

28   This is a quote from McCarthy's book on Tintin. Yet in marked
      contrast to McCarthy, Hergé didn't actually sign with his real
      name when copyrighting his Tintin cartoons. As McCarthy
      acknowledges: 'His very name, or rather *nom de plume*, was
      born from a double-move of covering up and rewriting: taking
      the initials of his real name Georges Remi, he reversed them
      into RG or, written as this is pronounced in French, Hergé. In
      using this word as his signature, he hid even as he made him-
      self most public' (McCarthy 2006).

29   Borschke identifies two other problems with Lessig's ap-
      proach to remix that could also be raised with regards to that
      of McCarthy. 'First, it conflates remixing with the technique
      of sampling – that is, isolating a fragment of some media
      source, or quoting it, within the mixing of layers. Second, if
      we consider the musical practice of remixing, we find that it
      is not necessarily dependent on quotation as such. When a
      remixer drops out the vocals, filters the horn sounds, or adds
      a percussion track, they are not referencing the tracks that
      make up the song, but using them differently (or not at all).
      Remixing doesn't have to be *about* the song; it can just be a new
      arrangement or iteration of the song' (Borschke 59).

30   For example, the author may be a means of responding to the
      politics of fake news and alternative facts epitomised by the
      regime of Donald Trump. 'How can one reduce the great per-
      il, the great danger with which fiction threatens our world',
      Foucault asks? 'The answer is: one can reduce it with the au-
      thor. The author allows a limitation of the cancerous and dan-
      gerous proliferation of significations within a world where
      one is thrifty not only with one's resources and riches, but
      also with one's discourses and their significations. The author
      is the principle of thrift in the proliferation of meaning. ... [H]
      e [sic] is a certain functional principle by which, in our cul-
      ture, one limits, excludes, and chooses; in short, by which one
      impedes the free circulation, the free manipulation, the free

composition, decomposition, and recomposition of fiction'
(Foucault 1984, 118-119).

31   To give him his due, McCarthy argues that the claim that
     should actually be made for Hergé is a 'more interesting one'.
     It is a claim that centres around two paradoxes. The first is
     that 'wrapped up in a simple medium for children is a mastery
     of plot and symbol, theme and sub-text far superior to that
     displayed by most "real" novelists. If you want to be a writer,
     study *The Castafiore Emerald*, and study it carefully', McCarthy
     proclaims. The second paradox concerns the fact that, as far
     as McCarthy is concerned, the below the radar space occupied
     by the Tintin comics is the 'zone where the real action takes
     place. Let's call it a degree-zero zone, a kind of loaded anti-
     space held in reserve. If literature itself has an ultimate truth,
     a deeper-than-trade secret either unexpressed or inexpress-
     ible, it is in precisely this kind of space that we should look for
     it' (2006). I will say more about the role such a ground-zero or
     degree-zero zone plays in McCarthy's work further on.

32   Foucault also draws attention to the differences 'between the
     proper name and the individual named and between the au-
     thor's name and what it names' (1984, 106).

33   McCarthy addresses this issue directly in *Recessional*. He ex-
     plains that the reason he refers to high-modernist works
     that were all authored by white men in this text (e.g. William
     Faulkner, Thomas Pynchon, Thomas Mann), is not out of a
     'placid conservatism'. Rather he is doing so in an attempt 'to
     tease out (draw into the light, Conrad would say), a rationale,
     or counter-rationale, working both in and, perhaps, against
     literature's very canon' (2016, 22-23). As we shall see, the ques-
     tion is: to what extent is McCarthy dislocating and disrupting
     the literary canon in working like this, and to what extent is
     he reenacting and reaffirming it, again and again? (I'm wait-
     ing before attempting to provide an answer. But if we wanted
     to be generous here, we could say that McCarthy's quasi-mod-
     ernism is suspended in-between the two; and that, like death
     in his reading of Hamlet, an answer to this question is reces-
     sive, messy and unresolved.)

34   A clear example of McCarthy establishing a barrier around
     his authorial self precisely to protect it and its autonomy from

the dangers of theory can be found in his 2011 *London Review of Books* blog post cum memoir, 'Kittler and the Sirens'. Here McCarthy recalls those occasions when he himself met the German media theorist in person. McCarthy acknowledges he'd 'heard all about Kittler: "Derrida of the digital age"', prior to doing so. 'While I was writing *C*, friends kept telling me I *had* to check out *Gramophone, Film, Typewriter*', the book for which Kittler is perhaps best known. 'But I held off', McCarthy admits, 'not wanting to cloud my primary research on technology and melancholia with academic "takes" on the subject' (McCarthy 2011b). For Justus Nieland this 'is a curious claim, not because it may not be true, but because McCarthy's work blurs boundaries between theory and fiction, and has never shied away from academic takes, as his superb 2006 study *Tintin and The Secret of Literature* attests. More uncharacteristically, it erects a boundary between the creative mind of the writer, inside, autonomously toiling at his work, and a buzzing world of thought and language outside that, McCarthy knows, is an unkillable humanist fiction' (Nieland 2016, 571). It is a less curious claim to me, however, given what I have already said about McCarthy's intellectual conservativism, and what I am going to go on to say about his dialecticism.

35 According to Zadie Smith, for example, *Remainder* was one of the best novels of the first decade of the twenty-first century, 'an avant-garde challenge' designed to 'shake the novel out of its present complacency. It clears away a little of the deadwood, offering a glimpse of an alternate road down which the novel might, with difficulty, travel forward. We could call this constructive deconstruction, a quality that, for me, marks *Remainder* as one of the great English novels of the past ten years' (Smith 2009). To be fair, Smith also locates *Remainder* and McCarthy – along with Melville, Conrad, Kafka, Beckett, Joyce and Nabokov – at the crossroads where the two traditions of realism and the avant-garde meet.

36 *Men in Space* provides one subtle exception. McCarthy addresses the theme of separation and disjointedness in this novel by inserting letters and reports into the narrative and by using multiple voices rather than that of one central character.

37 In *Pirate Philosophy* I try to encapsulate this argument by building on the work of both Derrida and Bernard Stiegler as

follows: 'because the human is born out of a relation to technology, and because time is possible and can be accessed and
experienced only as a result of its prior inscription in concrete,
technical forms, the nature of subjectivity and consciousness
changes over time as media technologies change' (Hall 2016,
59). I also argue that, while Derrida and Stiegler may understand this philosophically, they have difficulty in taking on
board its implications for their own work, which – like that of
McCarthy – remains closely bound up with writing.

38   For another account of originary technicity – one which, sim-
     ilar to that contained in *Pirate Philosophy*, is also a little more
     sophisticated than is provided in *A Stubborn Fury*, and yet at
     the same time intended as playful – see Hall (2002).

39   McCarthy's activities with the INS are more interesting in this
     regard. When delivering the 'INS Statement on Inauthenticity'
     at Tate Modern in 2008 he and Critchley replaced themselves
     with actors, for example. Making the declaration in New
     York, McCarthy and Critchley also stipulated that, 'like all
     INS propaganda' – but unlike McCarthy's copyrighted novels
     – the statement 'should be repeated, modified, distorted and
     disseminated as the listener sees fit' (McCarthy and Critchley
     2007, 3). For more on the INS, see McCarthy, Critchley *et al. The
     Mattering of Matter* (2012), a volume that includes a republished
     version of the INS' 'Statement on Inauthenticity'.

40   McCarthy dialecticism is also noticeable in the way he refuses
     to infringe copyright by stealing. As Smith notes, 'the great-
     est authenticity dreams of the avant-garde is this possibility
     of becoming criminal, of throwing one's lot in with Genet and
     John Fante, with the freaks and the lost and the rejected. ... For
     the British avant-garde, autobiographical extremity has be-
     come a mark of literary authenticity'. McCarthy, however, re-
     fuses to be 'authentic' in this fashion, as we have seen (Smith,
     2009). Yet neither does he rethink the relation between legal
     and illegal, authentic and inauthentic.

41   See my *Masked Media* (forthcoming) for more.

42   McCarthy has tended to experiment with the potential of me-
     dia art more when operating explicitly as an artist rather than
     as a writer. See, for example, the 2005 multimedia installation
     'Greenwich Degree Zero' that he created in collaboration with

the artist Rod Dickinson for The Western Front Gallery in Vancouver, 26 November, 2005 – 21 January, 2006.

43 Interestingly, Lin, Heti and Lerner, like Louis and Cusk (see n.22 above), are all associated with auto-fiction.

44 This is not to say that McCarthy does not believe in events: far from it. One account of modernism he provides is not as a 'movement, nor even a way of thinking, but an event: an event with which any serious writer has, in some way or another, to engage, and to which they should respond' (McCarthy 2007).

45 For one example, see *Calling All Agents*, billed as the 'first international symposium on the work of the top-selling author Tom McCarthy' (Birkbeck 2011). This event was held at Birkbeck, University of London on 23 July, 2011, and led to the publication of a book (Duncan 2016).

46 See, for instance, the 'Abolish Eton' motion that was put forward by the Labour Against Private Schools campaign group and passed at the 2019 Labour party conference. This motion also called for the removal of private schools' charitable status and the redistribution of their assets (endowments, investments and properties) to the state sector.

47 How significant is it that Stormzy's #Merky Books is an imprint of Penguin Random House, the same company that owns many of those responsible for publishing McCarthy's novels?

Works Cited

Acker, Kathy. 1984. *Blood and Guts in High School*. New York: Grove Press.

Adams, Tim. 2019. 'Kit de Waal: "Writing's Very Solitary – You Do It Because You Want to Find Readers"'. *Observer: Observer Food Monthly*, April 14, https://www.theguardian.com/food/2019/apr/14/lunch-with-kit-de-waal-novelist-new-anthology-working-class-writers-and-rights

Akala. 2018. *Natives: Race and Class in the Ruins of Empire*. London: Two Roads.

Allende, Sam Conniff. 2018. *Be More Pirate: Or How to Take on The World and Win*. London: Penguin.

Amerika, Mark. 2018. *remixthecontext*. New York: Routledge.

Armitage, Simon. 2020. *Magnetic Field: The Marsden Poems*. London: Faber & Faber.

Arnold, Matthew. 1869. *Culture and Anarchy: An Essay in Political and Social Criticism*. London: Smith, Elder & Company.

Authors Guild. 2019. 'Six Takeaways from the Authors Guild 2018 Authors' Income Survey'. *The Authors Guild*, January 5, https://www.authorsguild.org/industry-advocacy/six-takeaways-from-the-authors-guild-2018-authors-income-survey

Belgrade Theatre. 2020. 'A Statement on Eradicating the Use of the Term BAME'. *Belgrade Theatre Coventry*, July 16, https://www.belgrade.co.uk/stories/a-statement-on-eradicating-the-use-of-the-term-bame

Benjamin, Walter. 1973. 'The Work of Art in the Age of Mechanical Reproduction'. In *Illuminations*. Ed. Hannah Arendt. London: Fontana, 219-253.

Birkbeck. 2011. 'Birkbeck to Host First International Symposium On Work of Author Tom McCarthy', *Birkbeck*, July 8, http://www.bbk.ac.uk/news/birkbeck-to-host-first-international-symposium-on-work-of-author-tom-mccarthy

Borschke, Margie. 2017. *This Is Not A Remix: Piracy, Authenticity and Popular Music*. London: Bloomsbury Academic.

Bourdieu, Pierre. 2007. *Sketch for a Self-Analysis*. Chicago: University of Chicago Press.

Bradford, Richard. 2018. 'Review of *Literary Studies Deconstructed: A Polemic* by Catherine Butler'. *Times Higher Education*, October 18, https://www.timeshighereducation.com/books/literary-studies-deconstructed-polemic-catherine-butler-palgrave

Bragg, Melvyn. 1969. *The Hired Man*. London: Secker & Warburg.

Bragg, Melvyn. 1970. *A Place in England*. London: Secker & Warburg.

Bragg, Melvyn. 1980. *Kingdom Come*. London: Secker & Warburg.

Brouillette, Sarah. 2014. *Literature and the Creative Economy*. Stanford: Stanford University Press.

Centre for Literacy in Primary Education. 2018. *Reflecting Realities - Survey of Ethnic Representation within UK Children's Literature 2017*, July, https://clpe.org.uk/library-and-resources/research/reflecting-realities-survey-ethnic-representation-within-uk-children

Centre for Literacy in Primary Education. 2019. *Reflecting Realities – Survey of Ethnic Representation within UK Children's Literature 2018*, September, https://clpe.org.uk/library-and-resources/research/reflecting-realities-survey-ethnic-representation-within-uk-children

#CharitySoWhite. 2020. 'Racial Injustice in the Covid-19 Response: A Live Position Paper'. *Charity So White*, April 19, https://charitysowhite.org/covid19

Cramer, Florian. 2014. 'What Is "Post-Digital"?'. *APRJA*, Vol. 3, Issue 1, https://aprja.net/article/view/116068

Cullinane, Carl and Rebecca Montacute. 2020. *Impact Brief: School Shutdown*. Sutton Trust, April 20, https://www.suttontrust.com/our-research/covid-19-and-social-mobility-impact-brief

Cummings, Dominic. 2020. '"Two Hands are a Lot" – We're Hiring Data Scientists, Project Managers, Policy Experts, Assorted Weirdos....'. *Dominic Cummings' blog*, January 2, https://dominiccummings.com/2020/01/02/two-hands-are-a-lot-were-hiring-data-scientists-project-managers-policy-experts-assorted-weirdos

De Lagasnerie, Geoffroy and Édouard Louis. 2015. 'Manifesto for an Intellectual and Political Counteroffensive'. *Los Angeles Review of Books*, October 25, https://lareviewofbooks.org/article/manifesto-for-an-intellectual-and-political-counter-offensive

De Waal, Kit. Ed. 2019. *Common People: An Anthology of Working Class Writers*. London: Unbound.

Derrida, Jacques. 1995. 'The Rhetoric of Drugs', In *Points ... Interviews, 1974-1994*. Ed. Elizabeth Weber. Stanford: Stanford University Press.

Drąg, Wojciech. 2019. 'The Goldsmiths Prize and its Conceptualization of Experimental Literature'. Polish Journal of English Studies, Volume 5, Issue 1, 35-55.

Duncan, Dennis. Ed. 2016. *Tom McCarthy: Critical Essays*. Canterbury: Glyphi.

Eddo-Lodge, Reni. 2017. *Why I'm No Longer Talking to White People About Race*. London: Bloomsbury.

Ellmann, Lucy. 2019. *Ducks, Newburyport*. Norwich: Galley Beggar Press.

Eribon, Didier. 1992. *Michel Foucault*. London: Faber & Faber.

Eribon, Didier. 1994. *Michel Foucault et ses contemporains*. Paris: Fayard.

Eribon, Didier. 2013. *Returning To Reims*. Los Angeles: Semiotext(e).

Eribon, Didier. 2018. *Returning To Reims*. London: Allen Lane.

Evaristo, Bernadine. 2019. *Girl, Woman, Other*. London: Hamish Hamilton

Foer, Jonathan Safran. 2010. *Tree of Codes*. London: Visual Editions.

Foucault, Michel. 1980. 'The Confession of the Flesh'. In *Power/Knowledge: Selected Interviews and Other Writings, 1972-1977*. Ed. Colin Gordon. New York: Pantheon Books, 194-228.

Foucault, Michel. 1984. 'What Is an Author?'. In *The Foucault Reader*. Ed. Paul Rabinow. Harmondsworth: Penguin.

Freeman Hadley. 2014. 'The Latest Message
for Female Writers – Don't Think, Just Spill'.
The Guardian, September 19, https://www.
theguardian.com/commentisfree/2014/sep/19/
female-writers-lena-dunham-publishers-memoirs

Freeman, Hadley. 2020. *House Of Glass: The Story and
Secrets of a Twentieth-Century Jewish Family*. New York:
HarperCollins.

Freud, Sigmund. 1917. 'Mourning and Melancholia'. In
*The Standard Edition of The Complete Psychological Works
of Sigmund Freud*, Volume 14. London: Hogarth Press,
243-258.

Friedman, Sam and Daniel Laurison. 2019. *The Class
Ceiling: Why It Pays to Be Privileged*. London: Policy
Press.

Green, Francis and David Kynaston. 2019. *Engines
of Privilege: Britain's Private School Problem*. London:
Bloomsbury.

Hall, Gary. 2002. 'Para-site'. In *The Cyborg Experiments:
The Extensions of the Body in the Media Age*. Ed. Joanna
Zylinska. Continuum: London and New York,
131-146.

Hall, Gary. 2009. 'Pirate Philosophy 1.0'. *Culture
Machine*, Vol. 10, https://culturemachine.net/
wp-content/uploads/2019/01/344-746-1-PB.pdf

Hall, Gary. 2016. *Pirate Philosophy*. Cambridge, MA: MIT
Press.

Hall, Gary. 2017. *The Inhumanist Manifesto: Extended Play*. Boulder: The Techne Lab, http://art.colorado.edu/ research/Hall_Inhumanist-Manifesto.pdf

Hall, Gary. 2019. 'Anti-Bourgeois Theory'. *Media Theory*, Vol. 3, No. 2. December, http://journalcontent. mediatheoryjournal.org/index.php/mt/article/ view/91

Hallberg, Garth Risk. 2011. 'How Avant Is It? Zadie Smith, Tom McCarthy, and the Novel's Way Forward'. *The Millions*, April 19, https://themillions. com/2011/04/how-avant-is-it-zadie-smith-tom-mccarthy-and-the-novel's-way-forward.html

Hayles, N. Katherine. 2017. 'The Costs of Consciousness: Tom McCarthy's *Remainder* and Peter Watts's *Blindsight*'. In *Unthought: The Power of the Cognitive Unconscious*. Chicago and London: University of Chicago Press, 86-111.

Jennings, Jeremy. 2002. 'Deaths of the Intellectual: A Comparative Autopsy'. In *The Public Intellectual*. Ed. Helen Small. Oxford: Blackwell, 110-130.

Johnson, B.S. 1969. *The Unfortunates*. London: Secker & Warburg.

Josipovici, Gabriel. 2010. *What Ever Happened to Modernism?*. New Haven: Yale University Press.

Joyce, Robert and Xiaowei Xu. 2020. *Sector Shutdowns During the Coronavirus Crisis: Which Workers Are Most Exposed?*. Institute of Fiscal Studies, April 6, https:// www.ifs.org.uk/publications/14791

Kachka, Boris. 2015. 'Tom McCarthy Goes to TED'. *Vulture*, February 12, https://www.vulture.com/2015/02/tom-mccarthy-goes-to-ted.html

Kelly, Stuart. 2016. 'Does *Westworld* Tell a Truer Story than the Novel Can?' *The Guardian*, December 20, https://www.theguardian.com/books/booksblog/2016/dec/20/does-westworld-tell-a-truer-story-than-a-novel-can

Kirby, Philip. 2016. *Leading People 2016*. Sutton Trust, February 24, https://www.suttontrust.com/our-research/leading-people-2016-education-background

Lammy, David. 2017. 'Oxbridge Access Data'. *David Lammy*, October 20, https://www.davidlammy.co.uk/single-post/2017/10/20/Oxbridge-access-data

Lamont, Michèle. 1987. 'How to Become a Dominant French Philosopher: The Case of Jacques Derrida'. *American Journal of Sociology*, Vol. 93, No. 3, 584-622.

Le Monde in English. 2018. 'Édouard Louis: Life with his Brothers in Arms and in Spirit'. *Medium*, August 17, https://medium.com/m-le-magazine-du-monde/edouard-louis-life-with-his-brothers-in-arms-and-in-spirit-99951352c1c2

Lessig, Lawrence. 2008. *Remix: Making Art and Commerce Thrive in the Hybrid Economy*. London: Bloomsbury.

Louis, Édouard. 2013. *Pierre Bourdieu. L'insoumission en heritage*. Paris: Presses Universitaires de France.

Louis, Édouard. 2017. *The End of Eddy*. London: Vintage.

Louis, Édouard. 2018. *History of Violence*. London: Harvill Secker.

Louis, Édouard. 2019a. 'Toni Morrison Remembered by Édouard Louis: "Her Laugh Was Her Revenge Against The World"'. *The Guardian*, August 11, https://www.theguardian.com/books/2019/aug/11/toni-morrison-remembered-by-edouard-louis

Louis, Édouard. 2019b. *Who Killed My Father?* London: Harvill Secker.

Mance, Henry. 2016. 'Britain Has Had Enough of Experts, Says Gove', *Financial Times*, June 3, https://www.ft.com/content/3be49734-29cb-11e6-83e4-abc22d5d108c

Mason, Matt. 2008. *The Pirate's Dilemma: How Hackers, Punk Capitalists and Graffiti Millionaires Are Remixing our Culture and Changing the World*. London: Allen Lane.

McBride, Eimear. 2013. *A Girl Is a Half-Formed Thing*. Norwich: Galley Beggar Press.

McCarthy, Tom and Simon Critchley. 2007. 'The New York Declaration: INS Statement on Inauthenticity'. International Necronautical Society (INS), September 25, 1-20.

McCarthy, Tom, Simon Critchley *et al.* 2012. *The Mattering of Matter: Documents from the Archive of the International Necronautical Society.* Berlin: Sternberg Press.

McCarthy, Tom. 2006. *Tintin and The Secret of Literature.* London: Granta Books, electronic edition, n. pag.

McCarthy, Tom. 2007. 'Tom McCarthy's Top 10 European Modernists'. *The Guardian,* May 8, https://www.theguardian.com/books/2007/may/08/top10.modernists

McCarthy, Tom. 2010. *C.* New York: Alfred A. Knopf.

McCarthy, Tom. 2011a. 'David Foster Wallace: The Last Audit'. *New York Times,* April 14, https://www.nytimes.com/2011/04/17/books/review/book-review-the-pale-king-by-david-foster-wallace.html

McCarthy, Tom. 2011b. 'Kittler and the Sirens'. *London Review of Books: LRB blog,* November 9, https://www.lrb.co.uk/blog/2011/november/kittler-and-the-sirens

McCarthy, Tom. 2012. *Transmission and the Individual Remix: How Literature Works.* New York: Vintage Books, electronic edition, n. pag.

McCarthy, Tom. 2015a. *Remainder.* Surrey: Alma Books Ltd. (First published in 2005.)

McCarthy, Tom. 2015b. *Satin Island.* London: Vintage.

McCarthy, Tom. 2016. *Recessional – or, The Time of the Hammer.* Zurich-Berlin: diaphanes.

McCarthy, Tom. 2017. *Typewriters, Bombs, Jellyfish: Essays.* New York: New York Review of Books.

McGarvey, Darren. 2018. *Poverty Safari: Understanding the Anger of Britain's Underclass.* London: Picador.

Montacute, Rebecca and Carl Cullinane. 2018. *Access to Advantage: The Influence of School and Place on Admissions to Top Universities.* Sutton Trust, December 7, https://www.suttontrust.com/wp-content/uploads/2019/12/AccesstoAdvantage-2018.pdf

Mouffe, Chantal. 2013. *Agonistics: Thinking the World Politically.* London: Verso.

Nieland, Justus. 2012. 'Dirty Media: Tom McCarthy and the Afterlife of Modernism'. *MFS: Modern Fiction Studies*, Vol. 58, no 3, Fall, 569-599.

Nilsson, Magnus and John Lennon. Eds. 2017. *Working-Class Literature(s): Historical and International Perspectives.* Stockholm: Stockholm University Press.

Ofcom. 2019. *Diversity and Equal Opportunities in Television,* September 18, https://www.ofcom.org.uk/tv-radio-and-on-demand/information-for-industry/guidance/diversity/diversity-equal-opportunities-television

Office of National Statistics. 2020a. *Coronavirus (COVID-19) Related Deaths by Ethnic Group, England and Wales: 2 March 2020 to 10 April 2020*, May 7, https://www.ons.gov.uk/peoplepopulationandcommunity/birthsdeathsandmarriages/deaths/articles/coronavirusrelateddeathsbyethnicgroupenglandandwales/2march2020to10april2020

Office of National Statistics. 2020b. *Coronavirus (COVID-19) Related Deaths By Occupation, England and Wales: Deaths Registered Up to and Including 20 April 2020*, May 11, https://www.ons.gov.uk/peoplepopulationandcommunity/healthandsocialcare/causesofdeath/bulletins/covid19relateddeathsbyoccupationenglandandwales/deathsregistereduptoandincluding20april2020#men-and-coronavirus-related-deaths-by-occupation

Paine, Andre. 2018. 'Q&A: Enjoying the Good Life (Festival) with Cerys Matthews'. *Music Week*, September 14, https://www.musicweek.com/live/read/q-a-enjoying-the-good-life-festival-with-cerys-matthews/073817

Publishers Association. 2020a. 'Diversity Survey of the Publishing Workforce 2019'. *Publishers Association*, January 24, https://www.publishers.org.uk/publications/diversity-survey-of-the-publishing-workforce-2019/

Publishers Association. 2020b. *UK Publishing Industry Diversity & Inclusion Survey 2019*, https://www. publishers.org.uk/wp-content/uploads/2020/03/ Diversity-Survey-of-Publishing-Workforce-2019.pdf

Reeves, Aaron and Sam Friedman. 2017. 'The Decline and Persistence of the Old Boy: Private Schools and Elite Recruitment 1897-2016'. *American Sociological Review*, Vol. 82, Issue 6, 1139-1166.

Renton, Alex. 2017. *Stiff Upper Lip: Secrets, Crimes and the Schooling of a Ruling Class*. London: Weidenfeld & Nicolson.

Rose, Mark. 1993. *Authors and Owners: The Invention of Copyright*. Cambridge, MA and London: Harvard University Press.

Rourke, Lee and Tom McCarthy. 2009. '"I Suppose You Could View What I Do as a Kind of Grand Anti-Humanist Manifesto"'. *The Guardian*, September 18, https://www.theguardian.com/books/2010/sep/18/ tom-mccarthy-lee-rourke-conversation

Royal Society of Literature. 2019. *A Room of My Own: What Writers Need to Work Today*, June, https:// rsliterature.org/wp-content/uploads/2019/06/RSL-A-Room-of-My-Own-Report-19-June-2019.pdf

Saporta, Marc. 2011. *Composition No.1*. London: Visual Editions. (First published in 1962.)

Schulz, Bruno. 1988. *The Street of Crocodiles and Sanatorium Under the Sign of the Hourglass*. London: Picador. (First published in 1934.)

Schwartz, Alexandra. 2018. 'To Exist in the Eyes of Others: An Interview with the Novelist Édouard Louis on the Gilets Jaunes Movement'. *The New Yorker,* December 14, https://www.newyorker.com/news/news-desk/to-exist-in-the-eyes-of-others-an-interview-with-the-novelist-edouard-louis-on-the-gilets-jaunes-movement

Shaffi, Sarah. 2016. 'Publishing Seeks to Address Industry's Lack of Diversity'. *The Bookseller,* November 4, https://www.thebookseller.com/news/publishing-seeks-address-industry-s-lack-diversity-426031

Smith, Ali. 2015. *How to Be Both.* London: Penguin.

Smith, Zadie. 2009. 'Two Directions for the Novel'. In *Changing My Mind: Occasional Essays.* New York: Penguin, electronic edition, n. pag.

Smith, Zadie. 2010. 'Generation Why?'. *New York Review of Books,* November 25, https://www.nybooks.com/articles/2010/11/25/generation-why

Solomon, Nicola. 2018. 'The Profits from Publishing: Authors' Perspective'. *The Bookseller,* March 2, https://www.thebookseller.com/blogs/profits-publishing-authors-perspective-743226

Sutton Trust. 2006. *The Educational Background of Leading Journalists,* June 15, http://image.guardian.co.uk/sys-files/Media/documents/2006/06/14/Journalistsbackgroundsfinal.pdf

Sutton Trust. 2019. *Elitist Britain: The Educational Backgrounds of Britain's Leading People*. Sutton Trust and Social Mobility Commission. June 25, https://www.suttontrust.com/our-research/elitist-britain-2019

Taylor, Daniel. 2018. 'Broken News: Why Should Someone Like Sterling Be Seen as "Fair Game"'. *The Guardian*, December 10, https://www.theguardian.com/football/2018/dec/10/raheem-sterling-manchester-city-media-abuse-racism

Thirlwell, Adam. 2012. *Kapow!*. London: Visual Editions.

Thurman, Neil. 2016. 'Does British Journalism Have A Diversity Problem', *Neil Thurman* (blog), August 23, https://neilthurman.com/blog-reader/does-british-journalism-have-a-diversity-problem.html

Thurman, Neil, Alessio Cornia and Jessica Kunert. 2016. *Journalists in the UK*. Reuters Institute for the Study of Journalism, May, https://neilthurman.com/files/downloads/journalists-in-the-uk.pdf

Verkaik, Robert. 2018. *Posh Boys: How English Public Schools Ruin Britain*. London: Oneworld.

Waidner, Isabel. 2018. 'Liberating the Canon: Intersectionality and Innovation in Literature'. In *Liberating the Canon: An Anthology of Innovative Literature*. Ed. Isabel Waidner. Manchester: Dostoyevsky Wannabe Experimental, 7-19.

Wark, McKenzie. 2015. Preface to Tom McCarthy, *Remainder*. Surrey: Alma Books Ltd., vii-xii.

Wark, McKenzie. 2017. *General Intellects: Twenty-One Thinkers for the Twenty-First Century*. London: Verso, electronic edition, n. pag.

Wilby, Peter. 2020. 'The Expert in Social Mobility Who Says Education Cannot Make It Happen'. *The Guardian*, March 17, https://www.theguardian.com/education/2020/mar/17/the-expert-in-social-mobility-who-says-education-cannot-make-it-happen

Woolf, Leonard. 1960. *Sowing: An Autobiography of the Years 1880 to 1904*. New York: Harcourt, Brace & Company.

Lightning Source UK Ltd.
Milton Keynes UK
UKHW010639170822
407432UK00002B/506